THE COCOANUT GROVE
NIGHTCLUB FIRE

THE COCOANUT GROVE
NIGHTCLUB FIRE

A BOSTON TRAGEDY

STEPHANIE SCHOROW

THE
History
PRESS

Published by The History Press
Charleston, SC
www.historypress.com

First published 2022

Manufactured in the United States

ISBN 9781467152877

Library of Congress Control Number: 2022943537

CONTENTS

ACKNOWLEDGEMENTS

This book would not have been possible without the help of many fire professionals, Cocoanut Grove historians, survivors and families of survivors. My deepest thanks go to Casey Grant, Billy Noonan, Marty Sheridan, Charles C. Kenney, Jack Deady, Leo Stapleton, John Quinn, Jack Lesberg, Jane Alpert Bouvier, Paul Christian, Barbara Ravage, Kevin Richards and John Vahey for their recollections and expertise. I am grateful beyond words to David Blaney, who graciously shared his research with me; his meticulous work deserves a wider audience. Barbara Poremba was kind enough to share her research on nurses. It should be noted that Casey Grant, Barbara Poremba and David Blaney made major contributions to this book in the form of fact-checking and suggesting additional information. I am always thankful for the support of the Boston Fire Historical Society and its excellent web resources. Thanks to members of the Cocoanut Grove Memorial Committee, including Michael Hanlon and Kenneth Marshall. Special thanks go to the late Paul Benzaquin for sharing his memories of writing his landmark 1959 book on the fire. I also want to thank former Boston Police archivist Donna Wells and the late attorney Frank Shapiro. Thanks to Anne D'Urso-Rose for mental health information and links. Ronald Arntz provided me with some important photos of the club before the fire; I'm so glad that our chance encounter on a boat in Boston Harbor brought us together. I am grateful to Nora Bergman, daughter of Goody Goodelle, and Meg Schmidt, daughter of Martin Sheridan, for sharing stories of their families and providing fact-checking. Thanks to Kathy

Dullea Hogan for sharing the story of her father's diary, Joseph Short for showing me the wallet of fire victim Joseph Tranfalia, Ina Cutler for telling me about her mother's death in the fire and Jim Cavan and Phyllis Capone Cavan for sharing their family history. I must thank Bob Shumway and his daughter Jackie Sexton and son Curtis Shumway for helping me arrange a Zoom interview with one of the last living Cocoanut Grove survivors. I no longer have her name, but I am incredibly grateful to the woman who stopped at my yard sale, told me she had photos of the fire and shared them with me so I could scan them before they were donated to the Boston Public Library. Much gratitude to Aaron Schmidt and Bob Cullum for helping me obtain permission to use photographs from the Boston Public Library and the amazing Leslie Jones Collection. Gratitude to Donna Halper for her research assistance on the 2005 edition. Thanks go to the librarians of the National Fire Protection Association, the *Boston Herald*, the *Boston Globe* and the Medford Public Library. I am grateful for the encouragement and guidance from Mike Kinsella of The History Press, who has been unerringly patient and helpful, and to Abigail Fleming for her excellent copy editing. I could not have completed this manuscript on time without input from my partner-in-crime-writing, Beverly Ford, an extraordinary friend and editor.

PROLOGUE

Outside, it's bitter cold. Inside the nightclub, the joint is jumping. Anxious to take a break from the gloom of winter and the worries of war, crowds of people—young and old—hurry along Piedmont Street, in the city's theater district, heading for the revolving door under the Cocoanut Grove sign that reaches toward the sky. They anticipate the loud buzz of conversations, the cocktail-fueled laughter, the air saturated with cigarette smoke and perfume. They will check their coats and stroll into the main dining room, a faux South Seas paradise in chilly Boston, with fake palm trees, rattan furniture and chairs decorated with a striking zebra pattern. Maybe they'll be lucky—they might get seats in the area reserved for celebrities—a raised terrace set back from the main stage. Who knows who could be there? Cowboy star Buck Jones was in town, wasn't he? There was a new singer, too—Dotty Myles, only a teenager—but said to already be a star. Sure, it was expensive—an order of half a dozen oysters was $0.40, broiled scrod was $0.80, a baked lobster set you back $2.25 and a tenderloin steak cost $2.00. But it was the Cocoanut Grove, after all.

A night on the town. That was the plan for many Bostonians on November 28, 1942—that is, until they walked through the revolving doors and found the club too crowded for comfort and the heat too high for enjoyment. The coatroom was so full, coats were stacked on the floor. The dance floor was shrinking as waiters tried to squeeze even more tables into the main dining area. Disappointed, would-be merrymakers left to seek another club or restaurant or maybe call it a night. They would not realize until the next day how lucky they had been.

INTRODUCTION

The night of November 28, 1942, is seared into the collective memory of Bostonians. A fast-moving fire roared through the popular Cocoanut Grove nightclub on what was meant to be a festive Saturday evening, leaving more than five hundred people dead, dying or maimed for life. The inferno reached deep into the city's social structure—its politics, medical care, law enforcement and religious life—and touched nearly everyone in the Boston area that day, even those who had never set foot in the club. Mention "Cocoanut Grove" to most longtime Massachusetts residents, and tales flood out of great-uncles and aunts who died in or escaped from the fire, of grandmothers who treated patients as nurses, of grandfathers who fought the blaze or relatives who, amazingly enough, were at the club that night but left early.

Yet for decades, many victims and witnesses could not speak of what they saw or experienced; their silence has helped build a mystique about the fire, an aura of a catastrophe too terrible to imagine.

In sheer numbers, the Cocoanut Grove falls short of the devastating 1903 Iroquois Theatre fire in Chicago, which killed more than 600, and the collapse of the World Trade Center in a terrorist attack on September 11, 2001. But recall that the death toll of the devastating 1871 Chicago Fire, which spread over 3.3 miles, reached only an estimated 300 people. The Grove's impact extends beyond mere statistics. Doctors and nurses, faced with the medical battle of their lives, developed better treatments for burns and lung injuries—treatments still in use today. By listening to Cocoanut

The marquee of the Cocoanut Grove in the mid-1930s when the Herbert Marsh Band played there. *Courtesy of Ronald Arntz.*

Grove survivors, mental health experts gained insight into how trauma affects not only the body but also the mind. The fire led to tougher fire safety codes and more stringent enforcement of long-standing regulations. The investigation and subsequent trial defined the legal culpability of those who let expediency stand in the way of safety or do not maintain buildings properly.

Still, to dwell on the "good" that came of the fire does disservice to its victims and the lives of promise lost in a few moments of terror. Much about the fire remains a mystery, not least of which is this: How did it really start? Among its professional and amateur historians are Jack Deady of Bedford, New Hampshire, whose father, Philip Deady, investigated the fire for the state fire marshal's office, and retired firefighter Charles Kenney, whose firefighter father fought the blaze. These two men make it a point to warn fledgling fire researchers that the Cocoanut Grove is a story that never ends, that the fire has a terrible power to pull the curious into a labyrinth of outrage and subterfuge. Because many of those responsible for the Grove disaster took their secrets to the grave, there has been little chance to write a final chapter to this never-ending tale or find closure for the tragedy.

The fire's bitterest legacy is, perhaps, that its lessons must be endlessly repeated. On February 20, 2003, the Station, a Rhode Island nightclub, caught fire from indoor fireworks used by a rock band as part of its show. In the ensuing panic, one hundred people were killed or died later from their injuries. The tragedy's resemblance to the Cocoanut Grove was uncanny; in each, flames spread with horrifying speed, buildings were packed with patrons who jammed available exits and interior materials proved extraordinarily flammable.

The greatest temptation of tragedy is to infuse it with meaning, to promote the belief that something so bad must be a step to a greater good—or to see the unfolding of events as something dictated by fate, that mysterious force that seems to direct our lives. The heroics of the Cocoanut Grove nightclub fire have assumed mythical status, and the odd coincidences of luck are snatched up as evidence of divine intervention. But the never-ending fascination with the Cocoanut Grove does not stem from the heroics of a few but from the many strange threads of chance and circumstance that were woven together to produce one of Boston's worst disasters.

INTRODUCTION TO THE 2022 EDITION

When I first wrote about the Cocoanut Grove fire in my 2003 book *Boston on Fire* and then in a separate shorter book, *The Cocoanut Grove Fire*, in 2005, I thought I was done. I had pored over records, interviewed survivors and family members and drilled fire experts. Mindful of space and deadline, I wrote my copy and thought I would just go on to the next project. And while I did go on to other books, my relationship with this fire was not over. With an inexorable pull, the fire kept me probing its mysteries and exploring its lingering effect on New England.

Readers from outside Boston or younger New Englanders may wonder why one event—however horrible—has not only retained a grip on the city's imagination but also that new information continues to be found. I have learned over the course of writing eight books on Boston history that the past chases us like a dog after a speeding car, never catching up but never giving up.

Part of the profession of book writing today is lecturing on book topics and acting as a "talking head" on its subject matters. In the last twenty years, the more I gave talks about this fire, the more I learned about it. People came up to me with stories about its impact on their families and friends. In Boston, a woman showed me the diamond watch that her aunt was wearing in the fire; she died, but the watch survived. In Hull, an eighty-nine-year-old man spontaneously got up during one of my lectures to defend Stanley Tomaszewski, the sixteen-year-old busboy who lit the match that supposedly caused the fire. After a talk in Quincy, Kathy Dullea

A photo jacket from the Cocoanut Grove. A roving photographer would snap photos, quickly develop them and return them to the club for purchase. This was a common practice in many nightclubs of the era. *Courtesy of Kathy Alpert.*

Hogan read a moving passage from her father's 1942 diary that spoke of the despair at Boston College after its football team lost a key game to Holy Cross and how that loss shrank in perspective when the college community learned of what happened at the Cocoanut Grove later that night. After that same lecture in Quincy, more relatives of victims spoke to me. One was related to Eleanor Chiampa; at fifteen, Eleanor was the youngest victim of the fire. On another night, a man called me to tell me about the shame he felt over his father, who bragged about stealing from the pockets of the dead. He began to sob. I could not verify his story. But there were indeed press accounts of people robbing the dead and dying. All these stories gnawed at me. When people brought my attention to artifacts and photos related to the fire, I have tried to arrange for donations to the Boston Public Library or the National Fire Protection Association for additional study, thinking that another generation of scholars could delve into the fire and its mysteries. High school and college students repeatedly contacted me when doing projects on the Cocoanut Grove, and I've always tried to help them.

There have been dozens and dozens of people who told me of a grandfather or grandmother or great-aunt or uncle who intended to go to the club that night or who left early, sparing themselves from a ghastly fate. Not all these stories of near-misses could be true, I believe, but they reveal a greater truth—that nearly everyone in the Boston area at that time thought that what happened to the victims at the Cocoanut Grove could have happened to them.

The city continues to grapple with the history of this fire. The former Shawmut Street Extension, which runs through the footprint of the long-demolished club, has been renamed Cocoanut Grove Lane to commemorate the fire. Soon after the dedication ceremony, the small parking lot that was built over the ruins of the club was redeveloped, and a new, chic and expensive condominium complex was constructed. A memorial plaque, installed in the sidewalk near the spot of the revolving door for the fiftieth anniversary of the fire, was moved about a block away at the request of the condo developers, who apparently didn't want history intruding on residents. This somewhat callous act bolstered an effort to create an appropriate memorial to the fire in a nearby park that will keep the memory of destruction and triumph alive.

Over the last ten years, other authors have written extensively about the fire, including attorney John Esposito, who analyzed the legal ramifications of the trial that followed the fire in his book *Fire in the Grove: The Cocoanut Grove Tragedy and Its Aftermath*. A Texas-based playwright created a play based on the fire; it premiered in Boston in 2016. Most gratifyingly, a full-length documentary, *Six Locked Doors: The Legacy of Cocoanut Grove*, written and directed by Zachary Graves-Miller and produced by Graves-Miller and Michelle Shapiro, highlights the lives of those touched by the fire and the tragedy's lasting influence on Boston. Many other historians, both amateur and professional, have added to our knowledge. In particular, David Blaney has methodically and systematically created short biographies on the victims of the fire, and he has come up with what appears to be the final tally of the dead. Material from all these sources have been incorporated in this edition.

To be completely honest, I truly wanted to leave the Cocoanut Grove behind, putting aside its cruel twists of fate. When The History Press purchased the rights to my book *The Cocoanut Grove Fire* (originally published in 2005 by Commonwealth Editions as part of its New England Remembers series), I felt compelled to publish an update for the eightieth anniversary of the fire in 2022. In this updated edition, I hope to capture a sense of the lingering effect of the fire on the greater Boston area, a trauma that extends beyond the nearly five hundred deaths and the hundreds of injured. I can't do justice to all the victims, survivors, rescuers and medical personnel involved. What I try to do is highlight stories about key individuals to show the ripple effect of trauma over generations. Emphasizing how many survivors went on to productive, creative and amazing lives is a way to underscore the loss of so many others. What might they have done? Where would their life journeys have taken them?

One major new source comes from retired firefighter Charles C. Kenney Jr., son of a firefighter also named Charles Kenney, who fought at the Cocoanut Grove. The younger Kenney spent years researching the fire for a book that he never wrote. His papers and files were eventually donated to the Boston Public Library so this material could be available to future researchers. Charlie was immensely helpful to me during my research, and I hope to honor his memory by including some of his carefully gathered interviews and observations. I also seek to build on the work of other researchers who have written books and magazine articles and created presentations and web pages. All these experts on this fire have something to add to our collective memory and knowledge. This book is just one more part of a continually growing body of knowledge that will continue to expand as a new generation learns about the Cocoanut Grove.

1

BOSTON'S NUMBER ONE GLITTER SPOT

The squat tough little building, which is known on Boston's records as No.
13–17 Piedmont Street and to the wide world as the Cocoanut Grove, has passed
through successive stage of ambition, drudgery, prosperity and splendor....For
fifteen years, adults of all ages and fortune purchase illusion within its ornate
walls, pausing for a moment of artificial uplift before moving on again even as
you and I. Yet the Cocoanut Grove had another character behind its external
glitter, one that its casual patrons who ate $2 dinners and swallowed
50-cent drinks never saw with an outward eye. Behind the screen of colored
lights, soft music, pretty girls and moonbeams there was the moving shadows of
mystery which ran the full gamut of mischief, from swindler to murder to
questionable manipulation.
—Austen Lake, Boston Record American, *December 14, 1942*

In the early 1940s, Boston, the much-touted "Athens of America" and "Hub of the Solar System," had lost a good deal of its aura of intellectualism and Brahmin exclusivity. While the expression "Banned in Boston" would continue to be an operative phrase for the next few decades, the city was quickly shedding its prim and proper provincialism. The Irish political machine—nurtured in the first part of the twentieth century by the likes of James Michael Curley, Martin Lomasney and John Francis "Honey Fitz" Fitzgerald—dominated city politics. With a population of about 770,000, the city was segmenting into distinct neighborhoods, each developing its own economic and ethnic character. Due to World War II, which the United

A matchbook from the Cocoanut Grove reflects the tropical design and motifs that could be considered stereotypes today. *Author's collection.*

States entered formally in December 1941, the Charlestown Navy Yard was abuzz with activity and many young men in the area were preparing to join the war effort. A raft of newspapers—the *Boston Globe, Herald, Record American, Advertiser* and *Post*—fiercely competed to get the scoops of the day. Bostonians, like Americans around the country, were anxious to do their part for the war effort. *Life* featured page after page of war coverage, and in the fall of 1942, the magazine was filled with holiday advertisements for liquor and cigarettes. (With Santa on the box, "The famous Camel Cigarette Carton says 'Merry Christmas' in every flavorful puff.") Greer Garson was starring in the movies; Gypsy Rose Lee was on a Broadway stage. Nightclubs and movie theaters competed for entertainment dollars, families listened to the radio together and just about every adult smoked.

In 1942 in Boston, entertainer Mickey Alpert was Mr. Cocoanut Grove—not only because he once owned the place but also because his ebullient personality and natural wit as master of ceremonies made his name synonymous with the night spot. More charming than conventionally handsome and blessed with an ambition for the center stage, Alpert had

Right: Mickey Alpert was an ebullient entertainer who envisioned the Cocoanut Grove as the city's most glamorous nightclub. *Courtesy of the Boston Herald.*

Below: The popular bandleader Jacques Renard partnered with Mickey Alpert to open the Cocoanut Grove. *Author's collection.*

been the driving force behind the birth of the Cocoanut Grove. His dreams of bright lights and applause helped turn a former garage into Boston's number one glitter spot.

Born Milton Irving Alpert in 1904, Mickey grew up in Roxbury, where he worked in the furniture business. He started singing—mainly on radio ads for the furniture store—and acted in local theater productions. "I sold furniture in the daytime and broadcast at night. You might call it double in brass," he later told a reporter. The ambitious Alpert found a kindred soul in bandleader Jacques Renard (born Jacob Stavisky), an excellent musician who used a violin the way Benny Goodman used the clarinet. Renard had already developed a following in the Boston area. As his daughter, Edith Nussinow, said during a 2012 interview with this author, "Mickey really felt that Boston needed a very classy nightclub—a place where people could go dance. He contacted my father because my father at that time had the reputation for bringing people into the club. He had that expertise. My father had always wanted to have a restaurant and a beautiful club as well. And this was a great opportunity."

The pair's vision led them to an unassuming concrete block building at 17 Piedmont Street, just outside Boston's theater district on the edge of Bay Village, one of the city's oldest neighborhoods. The place had been built as a garage and was later converted into an office for a film distribution company. With legal assistance from Mickey's brother, George, then the youngest ever first assistant district attorney for Suffolk County, Alpert and Renard planned to turn the one-story structure into a premier night spot.

The pair got a boost when, vacationing in Maine, they met a generous but somewhat mysterious California businessman named Jack Berman. When Berman heard the young men talk about creating Boston's hottest night spot, he put up the money for the venture. Berman shared their enthusiasm for building a top-notch club, and money flowed from his wallet as if he owned his own greenback printing press. Reuben Bodenhorn, then a famed nightclub decorator, was hired to design the interior and the "look" of the club. Bodenhorn envisioned a tropical paradise to enliven cold New Englanders. He covered the walls with imitation leather or leatherette and dotted a large main dining and dancing room with fake palm trees. The main dining room featured a stage for the band and a raised terrace, made to resemble a Spanish courtyard, which would be reserved for important guests and celebrities. Hired as maître d' was Angelo Lippi, known as "The Count," or "Signor," whose waxed mustache and ever-unruffled demeanor in the face of celebrities or unruly drunks would become legendary.

The name and décor of the Cocoanut Grove in Boston was inspired by the Cocoanut Grove nightclub in the Ambassador Hotel in Los Angeles, shown in this postcard. While many postcards were made of the Los Angeles Cocoanut Grove, no postcards of the Boston nightclub have surfaced. *Author's collection.*

Berman reportedly spent $85,000 on the remodeling; he even suggested the name, "Cocoanut Grove," after the similarly named club in his home base of California. George Alpert, however, insisted that the club strictly adhere to liquor laws: setups were fine, but actual booze was not. Prohibition was the law, codified by the Eighteenth Amendment in 1919. But Alpert and Renard were confident great entertainment alone would draw the crowds.

Strangely, Berman wanted to stay in the background, leaving Alpert and Renard to take front stage, both as the managers and the main attraction. The pair thought that was odd, but as long as the cash flowed, they didn't question the largesse. Three days before the club was to open, the benefactor bubble burst. To their surprise and dismay, Alpert and Renard learned Berman was actually Jack Bennett, a partner in the Julian Petroleum Company, under arrest by the feds for manipulating the oil stock market and fleecing millions from investors. The Grove's munificent benefactor turned out to be a con man, anxious to launder his ill-gotten gains. Panicked and not even sure who owned the club now, Alpert and Renard called in George Alpert, who used his legal finesse to work out a deal to keep the club open. In a blitz of extravagance on October 27, 1927, the club welcomed its first customers under the title Jacques Renard's Cocoanut Grove. "The whole town turned out," as Lippi recalled years later. "It was Prohibition, of course, and we served only soft drinks," he added primly. "Setups at corkage prices were provided, however."

Despite the shaky start, the club appeared to be a success. Renard, a skilled musician, brought in the music lovers. Alpert added the pizzazz, winning acclaim for his stage style; newspapers called him "a second Al Jolson." But cocktails proved to be a more essential ingredient than glamour. Under the grip of Prohibition and particularly after the stock market crash of 1929, when the country really needed a drink, the club began to struggle.

Within two years, the dream had dissolved into bitter acrimony between Renard and Alpert, and the club teetered on the brink of bankruptcy. One of the issues appeared to be about serving alcohol; George Alpert was dead set against it, as was Jacques Renard, but according to Edith Nussinow, organized crime was somehow connected with the club and preferred that alcohol be a part of the club's business plan. For emphasis, "they took my mother for a proverbial ride. Put her in the backseat of a Roadster and covered her up with a blanket and took her for a ride to Revere beach. She said there were machine guns under the sheet with her," Nussinow said. Renard wanted out. He went on to help open another nightclub, the Mayfair, near the Cocoanut Grove. Eventually, Renard was approached by Eddie Cantor to be the singer's musical director and the family moved to California. Alpert also wanted out. Boston was too confining—he wanted to seek fame in the even brighter lights of New York City. George Alpert wanted to sell the club and be done with it.

Enter Charles "King" Solomon. A heavyset, round-faced thug called "The Capone of the East," Solomon ran liquor and dope smuggling and other businesses spoken about only in whispers. With his connections to the Murder Incorporated wise guys in New York City, he was untouchable in Boston, "short of a particularly messy murder," as *Record American* reporter Austen Lake later put it. Through his lawyer Barnett Welansky, Solomon made an offer to the Alperts that they decided they could not refuse. For $10,000, the club passed into Solomon's hands in 1931. Renard tried to put up a legal fight, but his stock in the club was judged worthless. The Cocoanut Grove became the fiefdom of King Solomon, whose backstory and style could have sprung from a Hollywood film noir script.

Charles Solomon was born in Russia and grew up in Salem, Massachusetts, after his parents immigrated to the United States. His arrest record dated to his teens, including a charge of helping to run a house of ill repute. Prohibition was a godsend to him and other members of organized crime.

Above: Jacques Renard and his orchestra, pictured on sheet music for "Just Call on Me." Renard was a popular bandleader who added cachet to the Cocoanut Grove. *Author's collection.*

Left: The visage of Mickey Alpert, dubbed "Boston's Favorite Radio Artist," used to sell sheet music. *Author's collection.*

Charles "King" Solomon (*far left*) was one of the most notorious gangsters in Prohibition-era Boston. A cunning underworld figure as well as a showman, he took over the Cocoanut Grove from Mickey Alpert and Jacques Renard when their mysterious benefactor turned out to be a fraud. Solomon was shot to death in 1933 at another club in Boston. *Courtesy of Boston Public Library.*

He eventually commanded a fleet of boats that brought in booze to the East Coast, guided by secret radio stations. According to Lake, Solomon had "a complete sideline of alki-cooking, morphine, heroin, cocaine and the dandruff-like little granules which produce delirious uproar. He hogged the bail-bond market, owned a large loan shark company at usurious rate, held full partnership in the white slave industry, along with a cut in a growing lottery racket and drivers and such like et ceteras built on human mischief." Solomon also owned (secretly or not) other hotels and clubs in Boston and New York City, but the Grove was Solomon's prized pet. "When 'King' Solomon ran the club, the sky was the limit in obtaining the best and the most famous in entertainment," the *Boston Sunday Advertiser* declared.

The best entertainers of the era came to the Cocoanut Grove stage: Sophie Tucker, Betty Grable, Gilda Gray (the original "Hula Girl") and others. Pretty girls were always seated at Solomon's table. Other stars who lit up the club were Jimmy Durante, Rudy Vallee and Guy Lombardo. "Sally Rand ran 'round without her rompers," as Lake quipped.

Solomon retained Angelo Lippi as the maître d', even though (as Lippi later said) Solomon could be slow with a paycheck and one didn't bother the King with something as trivial as one's daily wages. There were other dodges. Lippi was, for a time, listed as the president and treasurer of the club's corporation, although he later said he never attended a board meeting.

Texas Guinan and her *Too Hot for Paris* comedy revue was a favorite act. Known for her catchphrase greeting, "Hello, sucker," Guinan thrilled her audiences with her take-no-prisoners cheeky style. Lippi would later describe her favorite crazy trick. She would put a chair on the dance floor and invite someone there to answer questions from the audience. When the volunteer sat down, Texas would press a button connected to a battery under the seat; the shock would send the person screaming into the air. "Every show she performed, she would pull this trick. Most of the audience would be in on it, but there was always some 'sucker' who would go for it," Lippi told a Boston reporter. She called Solomon "Old Slobber Puss," and he loved it, according to Austen Lake.

One night, the popular racehorse Brass Monkey was feted right in the club, served some horse treats by Lippi himself. Aimee Semple McPherson showed up as a guest one day, and Lippi remembered her as happy and social, even bowing to the crowd when she was recognized. The next day, however, she declared in an interview with reporters that nightclub patrons should give up dining and dancing for the sake of salvation.

Whenever Jimmy Durante came to Boston, according to Lippi, he made it a point to come to the Cocoanut Grove. A big eater, Durante would also take time off from his meals to entertain the audience.

> Late one night, Durante ate a full course dinner, which included half a chicken. I thought that would satisfy him for a long time to come. But just as the club was about to close, he came up and asked if I could have another half a chicken. I stayed behind and had it done for him. At about 2:30 in the morning, when he had finished the second order, he asked for another half a chicken. I sent him to an all-night restaurant for that one.

Despite the genial face he displayed to patrons, Solomon was a ruthless, streetwise gangster. On January 8, 1933, federal indictments were handed down fingering Solomon as the "brains" of a $14 million liquor-running

The stage at the Cocoanut Grove in the 1930s. *Courtesy of Ronald Arntz.*

enterprise that smuggled whiskey to the United States from the Caribbean and Canada. After his arrest, Solomon posted the $5,000 bail and went about his business. "I have friends in high places," he told reporters. His darkest legacy—a tradition that doomed patrons decades later—arose from his deepest fears: he made sure exit doors to the club were locked inside and out so no one could sneak in on him and no one, neither patrons nor employees, could run out on a bill. Solomon's paranoia would prove to be justified.

On the evening of January 23, two days before he was to appear in federal court, Solomon, as was his habit, spent the evening at the Cocoanut Grove. His wife, Bertha "Billie" Solomon, was likely at home. He was on the outs with his main squeeze, a woman named Dorothy England, so he was accompanied by two young dancers and Joe Solomon, his bandleader (most sources say the two were not related) at the Cotton Club on Tremont Street, an after-hours club catering to Boston's African Americans. At one point, Solomon left his table to go to the bathroom and was followed by a group of men seated nearby. Witnesses reported hearing an argument, and shots rang out; the men fled, and Solomon staggered out. He had been shot four times in the chest, abdomen and neck. "The rats got me," he grunted before being rushed to the hospital, where he died. (His last utterance has also been reported as "The dirty rats got me," or, "Those dirty rats—got me.")

With mocking solemnity, the *Boston Globe* reported, "Bullets sang the requiem of 'King' Solomon yesterday and wiped forever from his face the smile that thousands knew." Throngs of onlookers crowded Fuller Street in Brookline to watch as his hearse passed during his large funeral procession. A passing onlooker might have thought a major Boston politician or religious leader had died.

As befitted a canny gangster, the fallen King was found to be nearly "bankrupt"—the final audit of his kingdom put its worth at only about $450. The Cocoanut Grove was listed among his assets as having "no value." Quickly—with a speed that intrigued later investigators of the fire—ownership of the club passed from Solomon's widow, Bertha, to Barnett "Barney" Welansky, "the bland monosyllabic young lawyer," as Lake dubbed him, who represented Solomon.

Welansky was, as reporters later wrote, "a typical American success story." Born in Boston in 1896, one of six children, Welansky grew up an ambitious, energetic kid with a yearning to be a lawyer. He sold papers to earn money for college and eventually got his law degree in 1918 from Boston University

The interior of the Cocoanut Grove in the 1930s. Note that the roof, which could be rolled back, appears to be open. *Courtesy of Ronald Arntz.*

and his master's degree a year later. After being admitted to the bar in 1919, he joined the prestigious practice of Herbert F. Callahan. Welansky's older brother James took a different route in life. James was a player in the city's nightclub scene; he was managing Boston's Metropolitan Hotel when a notorious racketeer and gambler, David "Beano" Breen, was shot to death in the hotel lobby in December 1937. James promptly skipped town, only to resurface in Florida two months later, claiming that he just decided to take a long-planned vacation—without luggage and under an assumed name. Arrested for the murder by prosecutors who claimed he and Breen had been running a gambling operation, James Welansky insisted that he did nothing and saw nothing, and a grand jury refused to indict him. By 1942, James Welansky was running his own bar, the Circle Lounge, in the Cleveland Circle area of Boston.

Unlike his brother, Barney Welansky tried to avoid connections with the criminal world. A bald, pudgy man, Welansky was the kind of guy who wore rumpled suits, not the tuxedos that Solomon favored. Years later, many of his employees recalled him as being personable and a fair boss. He ran the Grove like a business, not a showcase. Booking stars was secondary to making profits. He retained Rose Gnecco Ponzi as a bookkeeper. Rose's ex-husband, Charles Ponzi, had the dubious distinction of creating the financial scam that bears his name: the Ponzi scheme. Yet records were vague—deliberately so—on just who owned the club: the Grove's property was registered as owned by Welansky's sister Jennie and his brother Benjamin, who replaced Lippi as president in 1933. Barnett was listed as president-treasurer only after Benjamin joined the army in 1942. Welansky's business got a boost when Prohibition was repealed in December 1933. The night the first legal drink was served became legendary. According to the requirements of the law, the Grove could not begin to build a bar until noon of the same day the law was repealed. So work began at noon on a new bar off the main dining room, and by 9:00 p.m., the bar was ready—perhaps the fastest built bar in Boston history. Even as carpenters hammered in the finishing touches, patrons were toasting the death of Prohibition. Pressed to make his first ever speech, the suave Lippi put it simply: "The bar is open." Festooned with drawings of celebrities, the Caricature Bar, at forty-eight feet, was the longest in the city.

Shrewd businessman that he was, Barney Welansky didn't want the Grove's glitter to fade entirely. He brought back as master of ceremonies a man long associated with the Grove: Mickey Alpert. Alpert had pursued his show business dreams to New York, playing clubs and acting in a few Broadway shows. He had also met a blonde dancer, Katherine Rand, now his steady girl. But nothing equaled his early success at the Grove, and the Boston boy came home, where his smile and winning personality won back fans. Alpert worked with bandleader Bernardo "Bernie" Fazioli, who brought in a lineup of top-notch musicians. Other regular entertainers included singer Billy Payne, a good friend of Alpert's.

Barney Welansky turned the club into a complex. In 1938, he added the downstairs Melody Lounge, a dimly lit piano bar that retained a speakeasy atmosphere. He hired the club's original designer, Reuben O. Bodenhorn, for the work. Lighting came from tiny bulbs placed inside hollow coconut husks in fake palm trees for a sultry atmosphere. It was appointed with a circular bar with a revolving piano stand. Folds of fabric were suspended below a concrete ceiling to enhance the sense of intimacy; this cloth extended up the stairs leading to the main part of the club. In the main dining room, in an exotic touch, Welansky reconstructed the roof so a part could be rolled back on hot summer nights for dancing under the real night sky.

Welansky purchased two adjoining brick buildings, and on November 17, 1942, he opened a new cocktail lounge on the first floor, popularly called the Broadway lounge. The addition brought the total square footage of the club's ground level to more than 9,700 feet. The bland lawyer Welansky succeeded in turning the club into "Boston's number one glitter spot and the axis around which Boston's night life revolved," as Lake wrote. Welansky supervised almost every aspect of the club, arranging for all licenses and alterations and even looking for floor show acts when he was in New York on business. He had, in the words of attorney John Esposito, author of *Fire in the Grove: The Cocoanut Grove Tragedy and Its Aftermath*, made the club into a "respectable establishment" where a middle-class wedding party could be seated next to a family with teenagers in tow. Irish, Jewish, Italian and WASP patrons could mix. "Everyone went there." (Except for Boston's Black population, who were turned away.)

Even though Solomon had been his client and he served as one of his pallbearers, Barney Welansky tried to distance himself from criminal enterprises, although he did tend to ignore legal niceties, like proper licensing. Welansky knew how to work the system. A document from the Boston Board of Assessors the author found in the online Digital Commonwealth archives shows the property at 17 Piedmont Street was assessed at $120,000 in 1930, then $70,000 in 1938 and then $60,000 in 1941 and 1942. Nightclubs were, technically, still banned in Boston at this time, so the property was licensed as a restaurant.

An overhead shot of the club, taken after the fire, shows that it was a complex of different sections. *Army Signal Corps/Courtesy of Boston Public Library.*

Like Solomon, Welansky maintained limited access in and out of the club. Welansky's nephew Daniel Weiss, who was hired as a bartender in the Melody Lounge, knew nothing would upset his uncle more than losing track of his receipts. Cashier Katherine Swett feared his wrath—that fear would be her death. Like Solomon, Welansky seemed determined not to let a single patron skip out on a bill. And that meant keeping the exits limited. Customers had only one entrance into the main part of the club; they entered under an archway on Piedmont Street and through a revolving door. Another exit to Piedmont Street led from a cloakroom, but it was blocked by a coat rack. An emergency exit was located at the top of the stairs that led to the Melody Lounge. The door was equipped with a "panic" or "crash" bar designed to open the door from pressure inside the building. In the main dining room on the Shawmut Street side, a double door was hidden by curtains and a row of windows covered with wood panels. There were service entrances behind the orchestra stage that were kept locked. The only public entrance and exit to the new lounge was on

Broadway. A door that opened outward led into a small vestibule, and then there was another door, which opened inward. Welansky's existing liquor license was apparently extended to cover the expansions; according to Esposito, he did not apply to the building department for new permits. Why bother? He and his brother James were contributors to the campaign coffers of Boston mayor Maurice J. Tobin, an ambitious politician who was elected in 1938 in a surprising upset of James Michael Curley. Wrote Esposito: "Barney Welansky had made a simple business decision about the emergency doors. They were kept locked or obscured to discourage deadbeats from skipping on their checks. No inspector from the City of Boston ever challenged him on this practice."

On November 20, the Cocoanut Grove was inspected by Boston fire prevention lieutenant Frank Linney. His report said there were no inflammable decorations in the new lounge, the basement kitchen was clear and free from grease and there were a sufficient number of exits. He would later say he even held a match to one of the palm trees; it did not ignite. The condition of the club was "good." Eight days later, Linney's assessment would be proved horribly wrong.

2

THE COWBOY AND THE SCRIBE

There was a time when practically every boy in the United States would rather have been Buck Jones than president.
—Joseph G. Rosa, "Buck Jones Bona Fide Hero," True West *magazine, August 1966*

For kids around the country in 1942, Saturdays at the movie theater meant hunkering down with a mythical American hero, a gun-toting, range-riding, straight-shooting cowboy of the Western, a Hollywood-made fantasy depicting an American frontier that existed largely in the imagination. So-called B Westerns, often in serial format, roped in both young and old buckaroos who would spend a precious nickel or dime to travel back to a West that never really was. Of the many cowboy stars who galloped across the screen, few were more popular than Buck Jones. On November 27, 1942, the squared-jawed hero was headed toward Boston, not on his favorite horse Silver, but on the steel wheels of a train. Boston was to be the last stop of Jones's ten-city publicity tour to promote war bonds and generate publicity for his latest films. The stop would prove to be his last roundup.

Jones was then among the top tier of cowboy stars, along with Tom Mix, Bronco Billy Anderson and William S. Hart. Over the previous twenty years, he had appeared in about 120 westerns—both silent and talkies. Almost invariably Jones was the good guy, the man who stuck to the law but could right every wrong. While he had been eclipsed in recent years by singing cowboys like Gene Autry and Roy Rogers (a trend Buck Jones decried, saying, "They use 'em to save money on horses and riders and ammunition"), he was starring in two new movies for Monogram Pictures as part of its *Rough Riders* series. Jones had one advantage over other celluloid cowpokes: he had actually been a cowboy. Indeed, he once told a *Boston Post* reporter he got into acting by "an accident. I just happened to be around when they needed someone."

Charles Frederick Gebhard was born in Indiana on December 12, 1891. (There is some dispute over his birthdate, and his name is sometimes spelled Gebhart.) He grew up riding horses on a three-thousand-

In an era when the Western ruled the box office, Buck Jones was a famed cowboy star who starred in more than one hundred movies. *Author's collection.*

acre ranch near Red Rock, Oklahoma. At age fifteen, he lied about his age and joined the army, later serving with the U.S. Cavalry in the Philippines, where he was badly wounded. He recovered, did another stint in the military and later became a stunt rider for Wild West shows, a format popularized by Buffalo Bill Cody. While working as an expert rider for the Miller Bros. 101 Ranch show, he met a runaway and fellow stunt rider named Odille "Dell" Osborne. In 1915, they married in the ring on horseback; a preacher, also on horseback, performed the service. This was a partnership that would last for the next thirty years.

The pair later worked for the Ringling Bros. Circus and eventually moved to Los Angeles, where Buck heard that a movie studio needed extras for B Westerns, then being churned out factory style. However, he was asked to play a sheep herder. "I thought they were kidding me. You know a cowboy has no use for a sheep herder." At least that's what he told a reporter. What convinced him to round up woolies was the five dollars a day for the work. He continued to get extra jobs with the help of producer Scott Dunlap, who would later become his manager and one of his best friends. Producers at the Fox Film Corporation took notice, and in 1920, Gebhard became Charles Jones and later Buck Jones. He was billed as "the new screen sensation" as the lead in *The Last Straw*. In the era of the silent film, the six-foot, muscular, gray-eyed Jones made an impression. Other films followed:

A poster for *Silver Spurs* (1936), one of the 125-plus films—mostly Westerns—that starred Buck Jones. *Author's collection.*

The Forbidden Trail, The Square Shooter, Boss of Lonely Valley, Stone of Silver Creek, Ghost Town Law, Below the Border and many more.

By the 1920s, Jones had become a popular leading man and one of the country's favorite cowboys. Members of his fan club, the Buck Jones Rangers, numbered in the millions. "To millions of kids everywhere Buck Jones was the personification of the Hero, a fact that may puzzle this generation which has no time for hero-worship," wrote Joseph G. Rosa in *True West* magazine in 1966. Buck Jones Rangers' theme song said it all:

To the beat of the drums we're coming.
A million strong are we.
To the beat of our feet we're humming.
Our pledge of loyalty.
We are Buck Jones Rangers and we're swinging along with a song.
Yes, we're Buck Jones Rangers. Always ready to right every wrong.

By 1937, Jones had his name legally changed to Buck Jones. Yet unlike Tom Mix, off-screen Buck was a quiet, studious person. He rarely wore cowboy clothes in public because he felt it looked as if he were showing off, according to Rosa. When talkies (movies with sound) appeared in the 1930s, Jones was able to make the transition, and after a failed attempt to start his own Wild West show, he starred in movie after movie, including a few non-Westerns.

Ed Hulse, co-editor of the *Hollywood Corral: A Comprehensive Survey of the B-Western*, told the *Chicago Tribune* in 1998 that Jones "had an innate sense of what was dramatic. He brought sincerity and honesty to his performances. Moreover unlike some stars who stuck rigidly to formula, Buck wasn't afraid to experiment. He was an avid reader of Western pulp fiction, so he introduced diverse and varied elements into his films. 'Stone of Silver Creek,' for example, casts him as a good-bad man type who owns a saloon but who becomes a solid citizen."

In the late 1930s, as singing cowboys like Roy Rogers and Gene Autry began to win the West, Jones, now the owner of a California spread and a beloved boat, was content to ride off the range. He speculated that he might have to change personas to be the bad guy because the Western itself had changed. "A mandolin did it," he groused to UPI in 1940. "All these years I've ridden my horses myself without doubles and I've fought my own fights—at least twice in every picture—and now look what's happening to horse operas. They've turned into musical comedies—with chaps. And I can't croon. I can't strum a mandolin and I don't intend to learn. From now on, I'm a heavy." He was, after all, "an old-time cowboy, the sort the kids used to want to grow up to be like," as he told the *New York Times*.

In 1940, with the United States at war with Germany and Japan, younger stars began to serve in the military. According to some accounts, Scott Dunlap lured Buck out of retirement for a partnership with Monogram Pictures, which specialized in low-budget films, including Westerns, serials and other action movies. With Jones on board, Monogram launched a new buddy series with Jones, Tim McCoy and Raymond Hatton as the "Rough Riders." In November 1942, Jones and Dunlap embarked on a ten-day cross-county tour to promote buying war bonds and also draw attention to two new Rough Rider films, *Dawn on the Great Divide* and *West of the Law*.

About 10:00 p.m. on November 27, Jones and Dunlap arrived in Boston. Jones was tired. He was fighting a cold and was anxious to get home to California. But a cowboy hangs tough. He signed autographs for some servicemen when he got off the train and met his publicist for the Boston trip, a quick-witted young man with gold wire-rim glasses: Martin Sheridan.

Publicist Martin Sheridan accompanied Western movie star Buck Jones on his tour of Boston, including interviewing him for a local radio station. This is the last photograph of Jones ever taken. *Courtesy of Martin Sheridan.*

Ink ran in Martin Sheridan's veins. A skillful Boston-based reporter, he had a knack for writing personality features, particularly about the day's celebrities, from John Dos Passos, George Gershwin, Lilly Daché and fan dancer Sally Rand. Intimidated? Not this writer. "The bigger the person is, I find, the easier he is to handle," he liked to brag. In 1942, Sheridan knew all the media players in Boston, and virtually every reporter knew Marty.

Born Martin B. Orenstein in 1914 to a Jewish family in Providence, Rhode Island, Martin was an enterprising young man. He was a budding photographer and an avid collector of old newspapers, stamps and autographs. He mailed a request for a signature to famed novelist F. Scott Fitzgerald and finally got a card back from the author that read: "I refuse to give you my autograph." Signed.

Marty early on knew that he wanted to be a reporter, and he thought he would be better served by an Irish-sounding name at a time of overt and quiet anti-Semitism. In the 1930s, he had his name legally changed to Martin Sheridan. Sheridan was restless, ambitious and curious, jumping from assignment to assignment in pursuit of intriguing stories. He wrote for newspapers in Boston and Rhode Island as well as national magazines. On a ten-week trip in Cuba in 1940, he photographed Mexican artist Diego Rivera and interviewed and photographed Cuban president Fulgencio Batista. Sheridan wanted a Cuban flag in the picture, but officials searched everywhere in the capitol for the flag and couldn't come up with one. In 1938, he wed Constance Misslin, who would often come with him on his freelance assignments. When the war began, he wanted to accompany the military on an Atlantic Patrol boat but was rebuffed—later he would prove to be undeterred by military protocol. He wanted to join the navy but was considered 4F (unqualified) due to poor eyesight without glasses. In 1942, he published his first book, *Comics and Their Creators*. No writer had ever written a book on the comics, how the strips were created and how their creators worked. Sheridan knew many of the comic strip artists personally and professionally. When he was just out of high school, Sheridan worked for Russ Westover on his comic strip *Tillie the Toiler*, penning Westover's words into balloons, allowing the comic strip artist to get ahead in the series in order to take a vacation. Sheridan thought this book would be his ticket to writing success.

Despite the book, money wasn't exactly flowing in, and Sheridan had a wife to support. So, he did freelance publicity work on the side—he'd escort famous people around Boston, interview them on radio broadcasts and snap their pictures. Since he enjoyed meeting people, he didn't mind the work.

Once he even escorted the popular young comedian Bob Hope and wrote a long list of jokes for Hope, who may or may not have used them. And on the night of November 28, 1942, at the request of Monogram Pictures, he was to escort Buck Jones around Boston.

He had Buck's schedule completely mapped out: a visit with ailing kids at Children's Hospital at 9:30 a.m., Junior Commando rally at Boston Garden at 11:00 a.m. and cocktails and luncheon with theater people and the press at 12:15 p.m. at the Statler Hotel. Sheridan even arranged for the loan of a horse from a Boston police officer and managed to locate a Samson Spot twenty-foot lariat for Jones. Jones would also watch a Boston College–Holy Cross football game in Fenway Park from Boston mayor Maurice Tobin's box, do a radio interview and appear at the Buddies Club.

For Jones, the high point of the itinerary was wearing his ten-gallon hat and high-heeled cowboy boots and walking into a ward at Children's Hospital, where a four-year-old boy, suffering from temporary paralysis, forgot his pain and crowed with delight at seeing the big man that the nurses had said would come. It was all about his young fans, after all. He entertained ten thousand cheering youngsters at the Herald-Traveler Junior Commando Rally at Boston Garden with the horse and lariat Sheridan had procured. Dunlap and Jones then watched a much-anticipated football game in Fenway Park. But the day didn't go as planned—not for Jones or Sheridan and not for Boston College football fans. That afternoon, at Fenway Park, a crowd of more than forty-one thousand people watched as the unthinkable happened.

3

THE DEBACLE AT FENWAY PARK

This is Anything-Can-Happen Day. This is the day the unbeaten, Sugar Bowl-Bound football team from Boston College keeps its annual date with a buzz saw.
—Jerry Nason, "Eagles 4-1 Favorites to Beat Holy Cross before 41,300 Today," Boston Globe, November 28, 1942

Boston greeted the dawn of November 28, 1942, with happy anticipation. Despite the war and the early winter chill, this would be a day to celebrate. Today, Boston College's undefeated football team (BC) would play Holy Cross of Worcester, Massachusetts, in the last game of the regular season and would, everyone knew, win. BC officials were already anticipating a trip to the Sugar Bowl on New Year's Day and had planned a victory celebration that night. Bostonians loved their sports the way they loved politics—go big or go home. In the largely Catholic Boston area, a football battle between the two Roman Catholic colleges ranked with the rivalry between the Yankees and the Red Sox—the *Globe* even dubbed it the "Jesuit classic." The Boston College Eagles were soaring as the nation's no. 1 team according to the Associated Press, while the Holy Cross Crusaders were 4-4-1, a three-touchdown underdog.

Fifty years later, the *New York Times* called the game "arguably the biggest upset in college football history." According to the *Times*, when the 20–6 halftime score was transmitted by Morse code across Western Union wires, editors requested a clarification.

"You mean B.C. is ahead, 20–6?" they asked.

A poster of the Boston College/Holy Cross football game. Boston College and Holy Cross were fierce football rivals in Massachusetts. *Courtesy of the Holy Cross alumni magazine.*

"No," they were told. "Holy Cross is ahead."

And Holy Cross would stay ahead.

In the crowd cheering for Boston College was Edward C. "Ned" Dullea, a graduate of Boston College, class of 1923 and a center for the football team from 1919 to 1921. His was a BC family. His brother Father Maurice Dullea, SJ, was the faculty moderator of athletics for Boston College; Maurice had been captain of the football team in 1916 and led BC to victory over Holy Cross after a long drought. He was carried in triumph off the field. Ned's daughter, Kathy Hogan Dullea, still has the program for the 1942 game, with BC co-captains, Fred Naumetz, number 55, and Mike Holovak, number 12, on the cover. Ned Dullea was anticipating a joyous victory—one that he would write about in his diary.

Instead, he wrote: "Nothing in life is sure. B.C., number one team of the nation by the Associated Press national poll, four to one favorites for to-day's game, suffered the worst defeat of B.C. athletic history, being crushed by Holy Cross by an unbelievable 55 to 12 score."

55–12. A score emblazoned in the memories of the Boston College community.

"What happened," wrote Jerry Nason of the *Boston Globe* on November 30, "was that Holy Cross played the kind of football that Boston College had been playing for more than a month….The great Boston College line was reduced to rubble. It was mouse trapped and fooled and made to look bad by an offense similar to the one it had completely hogtied on other occasions."

Dullea was waiting for his brother in the Red Sox office after the game when the Sugar Bowl officials called. The invitation to play in the Sugar Bowl was withdrawn.

What was a tragedy for Boston was a cause for celebration for twenty-one-year-old John Quinn of Worcester, who had been rooting for Holy Cross. He had just two more days until he had to report back for duty at the U.S. Naval Training Center in Newport, Rhode Island. He had come to Boston with buddy Dick Vient for some rest and relaxation before shipping out. Thrilled by the Holy Cross victory, the young men arranged to bring their girlfriends to the Cocoanut Grove that night to celebrate. Vient brought his fiancée, Marion Luby; Quinn's steady gal was Gerry Whitehead, a girl he had loved since his junior year in high school. He knew they would get married after he returned from the war, and tonight they would be together at the Cocoanut Grove.

Many around the greater Boston area had similar plans. Saturday was a time to forget the war and the cold by going out on the town. And so,

Above: A fierce rivalry was played out between Boston College and Holy Cross at Fenway Park earlier in the day of November 28, 1942, with Boston College losing unexpectedly to Holy Cross 55–12. *Courtesy of the Boston Public Library, Leslie Jones Collection.*

Left: Bassist Jack Lesberg (*standing*) was in the band at the Cocoanut Grove; he survived the fire and went on to an illustrious career. He is pictured here with Max Kaminsky and Peanuts Hucko. *National Archives.*

Opposite: Singer Dotty Myles was hoping to launch her career with a stint at the Cocoanut Grove. *Courtesy of Charles Kenney.*

beginning early in the evening, people began to head to the movies, a restaurant or one of the city's nightclubs.

At the Cocoanut Grove, the staff of the club anticipated just another busy Saturday night.

Bernard Fazioli, the music director, was warming up his band of experienced and up-and-coming musicians, including Al Willet and Romeo Ferrara on sax, Al Maglitta on drums and Jack Lesberg on bass. Just twenty-two years old, Lesberg, a Boston native and the son of Russian emigrants, was following in the footsteps of his elder brother David, already a well-known musician. Lesberg played the string bass, then a relatively new instrument, and had developed a talent for jazz. After he cut a tour short with the Muggsy Spanier band to be with his ailing parents in Boston, he got a gig at the Cocoanut Grove, counting himself lucky to find work in the city's swank hot spot.

Boston was then a great training ground for many performers, including a number of solo singers at the Cocoanut Grove. Among them was Dotty Myles, a seventeen-year-old singer with a lilting voice and a natural, fresh-faced beauty who hoped the Cocoanut Grove would be her steppingstone to

Goody Goodelle was a popular singer and piano player who was performing at the Melody Lounge the night of the fire. This photo of her is at her dressing room at the club. *Courtesy of Nora Riva Bergman.*

stardom. Dorothy Metzger was born in New York City on West 101st Street; by age nine, she was taking voice lessons, and by twelve she was winning voice contests. In her late teens, she started singing in nightclubs and finally got the call she was hoping for—she would audition for Jimmy Dorsey himself. To prepare, she booked her first full-time professional appearance, a four-week stint at the Cocoanut Grove, beginning in early November. The reaction—from audiences and other musicians—was everything a girl could want. Jack Lesberg, for one, thought she had a terrific voice and she was a "straight ahead" hardworking gal. He also thought she was very pretty. Between shows, Dotty caught up on her schoolwork. As soon as she finished his gig at the Grove, she knew she would impress Dorsey.

A stunning brunette singer with a saucy style was preparing to perform in the downstairs Melody Lounge, accompanying herself on piano. Twenty-five-year-old Gorizia Maclone (her original family name was Maccarone) sang under the name Goody Goodelle. Born in the North End of Boston, she grew up in the Dorchester neighborhood. When they were children, Gorizia's eldest sister, Lillian, called her a "Goody Two Shoes" and the nickname stuck. Everyone knew her as Goody. Goody loved singing; she was a whiz at piano by age eight. She even taught piano and saved up her earnings to buy a baby grand. Even before graduating high school, she and her sister Riva began performing as a duo. In 1939, Gorizia adopted Goody Goodelle as her stage name.

For the previous two weeks, she had a solo gig at the Cocoanut Grove. Her mother, now a widow, didn't really like her working there. The Grove was, her mother thought, a place for gangsters. Hadn't there been a shooting there? But Goody liked it fine. She already had fans. A regular, who turned out to be an intern at Boston City Hospital, liked her voice. He would come in on weekends, nurse a Southern Comfort and Coke and request the song "Somebody's Thinking of You Tonight." A generous tip would follow. He was a real gentleman, that one. Not so much some other guys. So, she had been exploring the club—which she realized was a labyrinth of rooms—because she wanted to get to her upstairs dressing room without going through the main dining area. Someone showed her how she could cut through the kitchen to stairs that led upstairs. She was quite happy about that.

Other club staff were starting their shifts: cooks, bartenders, waiters, cashiers, cigarette girls and busboys. The chorus girls and tap dancers were preparing for the night's two stage shows. About ninety employees showed up for work that night. The club enforced an unspoken color bar: African Americans were discouraged as patrons, but at least three people of color were working in the club that night, as bathroom attendants in the men's and women's rooms and in the coat check room. As the short day eased into evening, patrons began quickly filling up the dining room, the Caricature Bar and the Melody Lounge. Others headed through the doors on Broadway to the club's new cocktail lounge.

Something of a Puritan mentality lingered in Boston. In the weeks to come, pundits and politicians seemed obligated to emphasize—as if to absolve clubgoers of culpability in their own demise—that the crowd at the Cocoanut Grove the night of November 28 was a "football crowd." As newspaper society writer Katherine Donovan put it, the crowd was "representative not of the night club habitue, the more or less professional thrill-seeker and spender, but a far more significant cross section of the average American boy or girl, man or woman." There were couples on dates, couples celebrating anniversaries and groups of friends there for a night of fun. Families brought along teenage offspring; maybe they were not thrilled to be with parents but happy to be in an adult place they had heard about. The club was licensed as a restaurant; technically, there were no "nightclubs" in Boston due to leftover regulations from Prohibition, so teenagers could enter without parents even if they could not drink legally. There were soldiers, sailors and other military personnel, many preparing for deployment. Each had their own, unique reason for going to the Cocoanut Grove that night.

John and Claudia O'Neill had come to toast their nuptials with their wedding party. They had been married earlier that day. They planned to leave after the first show, but Lynn Andrews, the club's roving photographer, had snapped their picture and they decided to stick around until it was developed and delivered. Joseph Dreyfus, a medical student and hardly a regular nightclub goer, was there with his wife, Adele, and another couple to have a send-off party for an acquaintance who was going overseas. Despite the disappointing game, Boston College equipment manager

A photo of a live radio show broadcast inside the Cocoanut Grove shows Mickey Alpert (*right*) and his sidekick Billy Payne (*far left*) cracking up on stage. Merrill, Richard. "Radio show at Cocoanut Grove." May 1941. *Digital Commonwealth.*

Larry Kenney was there with his wife. A few Boston officials were enjoying the club's hospitality, which often included free booze for local politicos. John Walsh, Boston's civil defense director, was with a party in the main dining area. In the new lounge, Barney's older brother James Welansky was sharing a table with Boston police night captain Joseph Buccigross, who was supposedly making his nightly rounds, and Suffolk County assistant district attorney Garrett Byrne, who would become legendary in Boston's legal circles.

Two key players were not there that night. Owner Barney Welansky fell suddenly ill on November 16 and remained hospitalized, recovering from a heart condition. With Barney in the hospital, James Welansky was there to, as he later put it, "look out for his [brother's] interests." The usually unflappable Angelo Lippi was home suffering from arthritis.

And there was one actual cowboy.

Sheridan's careful planning for Buck Jones took an unexpected turn; in the early evening, he, Jones and Dunlap taxied to the suburb of Newton for a

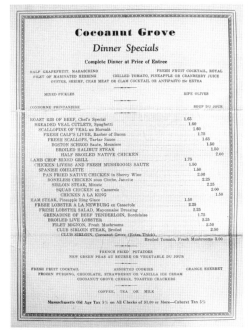

Left: The menu on the day of the fire. This was saved by a waiter who escaped the inferno and found he had it with him. *Photo by author. Item in collection of the National Fire Protection Association.*

Right: The cover of the menu of the Cocoanut Grove from the 1940s. *Photo by author. Item in collection of the National Fire Protection Association.*

cocktail party with local movie executives. Jones, now seriously suffering from a cold, asked Sheridan if he could skip his last obligation, his appearance at the Buddies Club, a serviceman's organization. He wanted to go back to his hotel and rest. Sheridan obligingly canceled the appearance. But the movie bigwigs weren't about to let the cowboy mosey along without getting a bit of his star power rubbed off on them. They had planned a party at the Cocoanut Grove and insisted that he come along. Jones, ever the stalwart cowboy, felt he couldn't let them down.

Sheridan, on the other hand, was grumpy. He had never been to the Cocoanut Grove and had no desire to go there. Still, he dropped off his camera and picked up his wife, Connie, who was happy about showing off her new mink coat. The group of about thirty people included Edward Ansin, president of Interstate Theatres; Philip Seletsky, head of the M&P chain that owned 110 New England theaters; Charles Stern, a New York representative of United Artists Corporation; and Harry Asher, president

The last page of the Cocoanut Grove ledger, kept by bookkeeper Rose Gnecco Ponzi, shows the amount entertainers were paid for the night of November 28, 1942. The ledger is now in the collection of the Boston Public Library. *Photo by author.*

of Producer Releasing Corporation. Most of them brought their wives. The party arrived at the Cocoanut Grove sometime before 10:00 p.m.

By that time, the club was so crowded that many people were either turned away or left on their own. Coats had overflowed the checkroom and were piled on the floor. Waiters were trying to accommodate more diners by setting up tables on the dance floor. The air was thick with cigarette smoke and perfume. Licensed to hold about 460 people, the club was filled with an estimated 1,000 or so patrons happy to drink, eat and escape the cold and the war for an evening.

4
INTO THE INFERNO

Getting out of that place…was like escaping from hell.
—*Interview with Anthony Marra,* Boston Globe, *November 25, 1962*

Marty Sheridan had not been to the Cocoanut Grove before, and he was not impressed with his first glimpse. The place was too smoky, too noisy and far too jam-packed. Sheridan's large party had to be shoehorned into two tables on the raised terrace, the section reserved for celebrities. The waiters couldn't even reach the tables; other patrons were passing drinks and dishes overhead. Dutifully, Sheridan passed the word that Mickey Alpert should introduce cowboy star Buck Jones, but he really felt he had done his job for the day. Pressed against a wall that seemed curiously warm, Sheridan ordered an oyster cocktail and hoped the night would pass quickly.

Above the babble of the crowd, he heard a commotion and the cries of "Fight! Fight!" Probably some football fans had decided to replay the game with their fists, he figured. Then he saw smoke and heard another cry, "Fire," followed by the crackle of unseen flames. "Let's get out of here," he said to his wife, keeping his voice casual. "How about my mink coat?" Connie cried. "To hell with it. Let's take our time and get out of here." As they and the rest of their party rose and started to move, Sheridan found himself engulfed by smoke. When the lights went out, Sheridan fell on top of other people around him and began to choke. As if clubbed with an invisible bat, he passed out, the shrieks and sounds of breaking dishes and

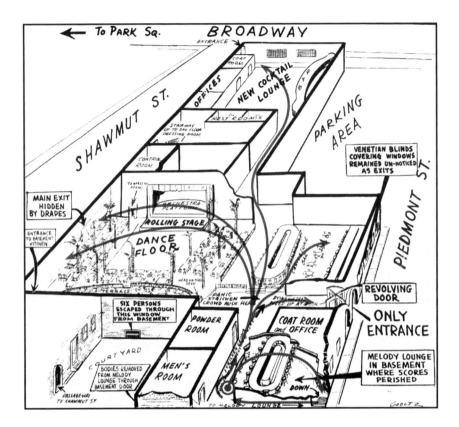

A diagram created shortly after the 1942 Cocoanut Grove fire depicts a cutaway view of the club's ground floor, with paths of fire spread added by *National Fire Protection Association Journal*. The circle at bottom center shows the spot in the basement, in the Melody Lounge, where the fire is thought to have begun. The arrows show how the fire spread through the Melody Lounge before shooting up the stairs at the bottom right and racing into the Caricature Bar and into the main dining area. *Courtesy of National Fire Protection Association.*

glasses growing ever fainter. He was vaguely aware that around him, people were falling, seemingly struck down by a ferocious heat that roared through the club like a fiery tidal wave.

Just a few minutes earlier, a man in the packed downstairs Melody Lounge decided he needed a little more privacy. His name has never been identified, and what happened next has been debated for decades. This much is clear. Shortly after 10:00 p.m. a man in the northwest corner of the Melody Lounge reached in to unscrew a tiny light bulb that was either in or near one of the lounge's fake palm trees; even the dimly lit Melody Lounge was apparently too bright for him. When Melody Lounge

The stairs leading up from the Melody Lounge. *Army Signal Corps/Courtesy of Boston Public Library.*

bartender John Bradley realized the light was out (or was informed that it was out), he told a busboy, young Stanley Tomaszewski, to screw the light back in and make sure it was on.

At sixteen years old, Stanley Tomaszewski was happy to have work. His mother was ailing, his father was unemployed and the family needed his wages—$2.47 a night plus tips on Friday and Saturday. His buddy Joseph Tranfaglia Jr., also sixteen, who worked at the Grove, had helped him get the job. Stanley, a football player and above-average student at Roxbury Memorial High School, was viewed as a good reliable worker, and that night in the Melody Lounge he was acting as a bar boy, serving drinks to people, despite being underage. Now faced with someone who had made the dim lounge even dimmer, he dutifully moved toward the table even as the customer told him jokingly to leave the bulb alone. Stanley climbed on a chair and reached for the bulb; he could not find it. So he took out a matchbook, lit one and twisted the bulb back into the socket while holding the match in his right hand. When the bulb was secure, he put out the match (possibly by grinding it with his heel) and turned away to return to work.

Patrons in the bar saw a tiny flare or spark immediately in the palm tree. Other witnesses reported seeing a flash moments later. Twenty-six-year-old Maurice Levy of Roxbury saw the top of the palm tree smolder, puff up and ignite, torching the drapes of material covering the ceiling. Both Bradley and Tomaszewski realized there was a problem, rushed to the corner and tried to extinguish the fire. Stanley beat it with his hands, but the flames were working their way into the cloth ceiling. Some customers thought it was funny, others were simply stunned and a few started to leave the lounge. Levy grabbed his wife and headed for the stairs. As the lounge rapidly filled with smoke and flames, Bradley and Tomaszewski started yelling for people to follow them into the kitchen—they knew there were exits there—as panic and confusion swept through the bar.

Behind the bar in the Melody Lounge was twenty-four-year-old Daniel Weiss, a medical student at Boston University and Welansky's nephew. He heard a noise and turned around to what seemed to be an unusual light in the corner. When he realized the ceiling was on fire, he pitched a mixing glass of water at the flames, to no avail. As people started to flee, he felt he just couldn't leave his post at the cash register. He dropped to the floor as smoke caused him to cough and gag. He soaked a bar towel with water and held it to his face near the floor where the air seemed better. The smoke had a strange sweet taste that made his nose and throat dry. The sounds of screaming grew louder and louder before fading away.

A ball of flame—described variously as bright orange, bluish with a yellow cast or bright white—shot up the stairs of the Melody Lounge and into the main part of the club. As much as experts can determine, here is the time frame. A small fire was seen in a palm tree in the downstairs Melody Lounge at 10:15 p.m. Within a minute, it had ignited the cloth ceiling of the lounge. Within four minutes, fire was seen in the foyer and Caricature Bar. By 10:20 p.m., fire was roaring through the main dining room and had reached the Broadway lounge. By 10:21, fire had engulfed the Broadway Lounge. By 10:23, the fire was advancing throughout the club. The fire not only spread ferociously fast but also moved in twists and turns. From the Melody Lounge, the fire barreled up the stairs, through the foyer and into the Caricature Bar and then the main dining room. It snaked through the corridors where only the staff was allowed, and into the new Broadway lounge, emitting a strange hissing sound, according to some witnesses.

Most of the crowd did what people tend to do in a fire—they retreated to the entrance from which they entered. That meant those in the Melody Lounge ran up the stairs, although some of the staff tried to direct them

The club on fire. *Courtesy of Boston Public Library.*

through the door to the kitchen. They pressed against the exit door that led to Piedmont Street, the door with a panic bar. It did not open. Dozens piled against it, beating on it with all their strength; it refused to budge. (It was later found to be locked shut.) Others made it to the top of the stairs and ran through the foyer toward the main exit, the revolving doors. Some foolishly stopped to try to retrieve coats. By now people in the dining room were aware something was happening, and many began to head for the revolving doors to leave. A waiter tried to stop them, saying, "Nobody leaves until they pay their bill."

As a crush of increasingly terrified patrons pressed into the revolving doors, it spun, ejecting some into the sidewalk. Then, as the crowd pressed on both sides, the door jammed. Levy, who had lost his wife in the crowd, managed to get out; he thought he was the last person to do so. When he turned around, the person behind him was being burned alive behind the glass.

Vera B. Daniels, age thirty, a mother of a young daughter, worked in the coatroom of the Cocoanut Grove, just off the foyer. An African American, she could not actually go to the club—that was the way of Boston, even though at this time Black men would courageously serve in the U.S.

military, albeit in segregated units. She was at her station when one of the managers rushed over to tell her to knock on the door of the ladies' room and tell them to get out because there was a fire. She obeyed, yelling "Fire" as loud as she could, only to be admonished by a manager to stop yelling *fire*, because "people will panic." It was already too late for calm; she was caught up in the rush of people trying to exit the revolving door. A flaming chunk of wood fell on her head, igniting her hair. She put her hands up to her head in an attempt to beat out the fire and then wrapped her hands in the pockets of her apron to ease the pain from the burns. Dropping to her knees, she managed to get out through the revolving door, crawling over bodies already piling up. Outside, she walked two miles to her usual taxi stand, but the taxi driver refused to bring her home: "You're going to the hospital," he told her.

On the dance floor in the main dining room, sixteen-year-old Ann Marie Clark may have been thinking she was one of the luckiest girls in the world. Her parents, Clyde and Mabel Clark, and the parents of her nineteen-year-old boyfriend, Fred Sharby Jr., had taken everyone from Keene, New Hampshire, to Boston for the day. Fred Sharby Jr. was one of the best football players produced by Keene High. His father, Fred Sharby Sr., wanted to show the young running back a college game. So, the Sharbys—Fred; his wife, Hortense; and Fred Jr.—and the Clarks piled in a car and drove to Boston for the Boston College–Holy Cross football game at Fenway Park. After the game, the party drove to Piedmont Street and went to the Cocoanut Grove for dinner. Ann felt so grown-up walking into the club with Fred and her family. After dinner, she and Fred got up to dance. The place was crowded, but that meant the two teenagers could hug each other closely. Fred was really swell, Ann thought. He was her first real first love. And then suddenly fire was sweeping over them, and they were in the middle of a panicked crowd. "Get down on your hands and knees and cover your face," Fred yelled. And that was the last thing Ann remembered for a long time.

Sometime after 10:00 p.m., Mickey Alpert, standing near the stage, was getting ready for the night's second show, which was to be broadcast live on a local radio station. He was chatting with singer Billy Payne, who would kick the evening off by singing the national anthem, when someone asked Alpert if he could announce that Buck Jones was in the audience. No problem. Just then, he heard a commotion in the dining room. "Hey Mickey, it's a fight," Payne said. As Alpert peered into the crowd, he could see fire coming into the dining room, and then fire seemed to be everywhere amid a swell of panicked screams. The fire spread like a shot. Zing! The next thing Alpert

A massive effort was waged to get people out of the club. *Courtesy of the* Boston Herald.

knew, he was downstairs in the kitchen trying to get out of the club. He did get out—he was never sure how.

From the stage, Billy Payne saw a terrific ball of yellow or white flames billowing past the checkroom and heading right for him. Payne attempted to calm the crowd, but he was pushed aside. Fleeing down the stairs behind the stage toward the kitchen, he covered his mouth with a towel as he heard someone yelling about getting keys for an outside door. As the smoke surrounded him, Payne started saying his Hail Marys, fearing the end was near. Then he heard the door behind the stage being smashed open; he called for people to follow him as he went upstairs to find a firefighter was pulling people out. "It seemed like a year, but it was probably ten minutes," he later said.

From the stage, bass player Jack Lesberg could see the commotion in the foyer, followed by fast-moving flames. Lesberg hesitated; he didn't want to leave his new, precious bass, but soon the entire band was fleeing. A drummer refused to leave until, with help, his drums were yanked from the stage, Lesberg grabbed his bass and joined the stampede, only to find himself stalled in a small room behind the stage that led to a back door, which seemed to be locked. As the lights went out, the room filled with smoke. Lesberg dropped his bass; he couldn't move and was pressed into a crowd with about fifty others, including Fazioli and Willet. Willet pulled out a handkerchief and pressed it to his mouth. "I guess this is it," he said to Lesberg before they both sagged to the floor. Lesberg was curiously without fear; everything was becoming hazy, and he passed out into a growing pile of bodies.

When the cry of fire rang out in the main dining room, Dreyfus, the medical student, stood up, because, as he later said, he was taught not to panic. He saw a sheet of flames coming across the room. Instinctively, he covered his eyes and almost instantly passed out. He fell to the floor and wasn't discovered for hours. He later woke up in Boston City Hospital, his lungs and trachea damaged and his hands burned to the bone. His wife was dying, as were many other people around them. By falling to the floor so quickly Dreyfus breathed cleaner, cooler air while the people who were with him got the full brunt of the heat and the fumes.

With their hair on fire and their skin blistering, people in the dining room scrambled for the only exit they knew, the revolving door on Piedmont Street. For many, that was a death trap. Across the main dining room,

Chaos outside the club. *Courtesy of the* Boston Herald.

behind draperies on the Shawmut Street side, was a double door. The wall on that side of the building also had three plate-glass windows, but they were covered with a wood veneer. A fast-thinking waiter wrenched aside the draperies and tried to open the door, which seemed to stick. People converged to try to open it, among them was John Walsh, Boston's civil defense director. They managed to open one of the double doors, and people began pouring out on Shawmut Street. Unfortunately, fire also seeks air. As oxygen in the dining room was depleted, the flames reached toward the air coming from the Shawmut Street door, turning the precious opening into a roaring blaze, trapping those inside who had not yet escaped. Among them was the young singer Dotty Myles.

The girl had arrived about 9:15 p.m. and thought she'd catch a few moments to study an algebra book before she went on stage. About 10:00 p.m., she saw a strange glow coming from the Melody Lounge and realized that the club was on fire. She could see the door on the Shawmut Street side and tried to cross the dining room to get to it. Someone knocked her to the ground, and before she could get up, an overturned table hit her squarely in the face. She blanked out and came to with the pressure of feet on her body, the heavy tread of men and the stabbing light impact of high-heel shoes. She heard moans, shrieks and someone calling, "'Mother…Mother… Mother." She was praying as she reached up and touched a man's hand and found herself yanked to her feet, her gown torn away. That was a blessing: she could see women, bright as torches, as their evening gowns burst into flames. She tried to follow the man who pulled her up, but he plunged ahead in the swirling mass of people. She pushed forward and fell into a sea of people that piled on top of her. She could feel the skin on her arms burning as if they were splashed with acid, and then she didn't feel anything at all.

Joseph F. Kelley, a building contractor, along with his friend Benjamin Wheaton and Wheaton's wife were having drinks in the Caricature Lounge when he heard a commotion and figured a fight had broken out. Then Wheaton said quietly to his wife, "It's a fire," and the three headed toward the passageway into the Broadway lounge. As panicked people blocked the way, Kelley was knocked down and lost sight of the Wheatons. He made his way through the passageway into the new lounge as the thick and oily smoke grew heavy and the lights went out. As Kelley later told police, "I felt a body. It was a girl. I picked her up. There was a strata of air under the smoke. You could see ahead when the tables had been all knocked over the stools. We picked our way over the stools. The crowd at the door pushed us out."

When John Quinn, Dick Vient and their gals arrived at the club sometime after 9:00 p.m., they managed to get a table in the crowded main dining room. A little before 10:00 p.m., after the guys had had a few drinks, they headed to the men's room. In the foyer there, they noticed the stairway to the Melody Lounge and walked down for a look-see. On a revolving piano stand, behind a circular bar shaped like a football, a woman was singing a jaunty tune with the line: "Never let a sailor get an inch above your knee. "Let's get the girls and come back here," Quinn said, "They'll get a kick out of this."

The men returned to their table and told their girls they had a better place in mind, and they all headed to the Melody Lounge. Once downstairs, the crowd was so big that people were lined up three deep around the bar. A bright light caught Quinn's eye to the left, and he saw a flame about eighteen inches high. It was either in one of the fake palm trees or in the cloth that covered the bar's ceiling. They had to leave. "You get going," Quinn said to Vient and Marion, "We'll be right behind you." As they started climbing the stairs out of the lounge, what appeared to be a waiter rushed by with a fire extinguisher. So it would be over soon, Quinn thought. Almost instantly, the waiter rushed back past them. As the foursome reached the foyer leading to the main dining room amid a crowd of increasingly panicked customers, Quinn felt a blast of heat sear the back of his neck. Turning, he saw a sheet of bright orange flames that stretched from ceiling to floor. He didn't look back again. Ahead, Dick and Marion seemed to have halted; he wanted to go one way, and she wanted to get her coat. Gerry asked Quinn, "Can I get my coat? "No," Quinn yelped. "If everything is okay, we'll get it later." Quinn knew that the main entrance was just to his right, but already he sensed people were backing up behind the revolving doors; that would not be a way to get out. And then the lights went out.

Quinn made a quick choice. Deciding that the revolving door would quickly jam, he joined the people who seemed to be pressing forward toward what would turn out to be the Shawmut Street door. He pushed Gerry into the middle of the crowd, hoping that they would be squeezed forward by the crowd. Grabbing Gerry by the waist, he whispered, "Do exactly as I tell you and don't say anything until we get out." Gerry broke that promise only once. They forged ahead into the mob as black smoke filled the room. They would take a step, then Gerry would trip over something, maybe a body, but Quinn did not dare to look down. He lifted her to her feet and rose, lifting up other people who had climbed on his back. He saw two men in tuxedos who seemed to be trying to swim out by pulling the hair of people in front

The window in the basement kitchen from which so many escaped, including John Rizzo. *Courtesy of Boston Public Library.*

of them. Quinn felt his knees buckling. Falling to one knee, he put a hand on Gerry's back, determined to push her out with his last strength. It was then she broke the code of silence. "Air," she gasped. Galvanized by that one word, Quinn pushed himself to his feet, and squeezed on both sides, he and Gerry were pushed out the door, landing on the hood of a car without touching the sidewalk. Someone walking by with a flask offered him a shot of liquor. Quinn and Gerry had only minor injuries. He did not know what happened to Vient and his girlfriend.

In an upstairs dressing room, seventeen-year-old Marshall Cole was killing time before the next show. A "chorus boy," Cole was a talented tap dancer who was enjoying his stint at the club; he usually went to the Melody Lounge between his sets, where his high spirits and ready wit were appreciated. That night, he was relaxing in his dressing room. He heard a commotion downstairs and figured it must be a fight related to the big game that day between Boston College and Holy Cross. He peeked down the stairs to see what was going on and was hit by a cloud of smoke and sparks.

He jumped back into his dressing room and started to gather up his tuxedo, his tap shoes and his pride and joy: his brand-new camel hair coat. And then a man—a waiter of some sort—came running full speed up the stairs, put his hands over his face and crashed through a large picture window at the top of the stairs onto the roof. Cole realized he had to get out—as fast as he could. He dropped everything—his shoes, his tux and his coat—and clambered through the window onto the roof after the man. He could see that the man was trying to get off the roof and that he jumped or fell into a parking lot below. For more than seventy years, Cole wondered if the man who went off the roof survived.

By that time, chorus girls, most in their skimpy performance outfits, were following Cole through the window onto the roof. Flames were shooting up both to the left and to the right—fire seemed to be all around them. Someone managed to find a ladder, but it fell short of the ground. Holding the ladder with another couple of men, Cole helped the chorus girls climb down the ladder; they had to jump the last six feet. Cole and the other fellows looked at one another—there was no one to hold the ladder for them. They did not realize it at the time, but rescue was just moments away.

Twenty-two-year-old John Rizzo of Revere liked both the money he made as a waiter at the Grove and the glamour of the faux South Seas paradise. The décor, he thought, was "positively beautiful." He arrived at the club at 4:00 p.m. to start his shift in the main dining room. A little after 10:00 p.m., he thought something was wrong. There was a crowd in the club's foyer near the revolving door. A fight, he thought he heard someone holler, "Get the cops! It is a jam." And then he saw flames. He started to run across the dance floor to the doors he knew were on the other side when the lights went out. The smoke was all around him, choking his lungs. As he got to the top of the stairs leading to the kitchen, someone pushed him and he fell, tumbling head over heels and landing on people below. People were now jamming into the kitchen area, all trying to get out. With another busboy, Rizzo managed to unblock a small window—there was some kind of duct in front of it—and helped people escape—maybe fourteen, fifteen, sixteen people. Rizzo was the last out, scrambling into a small courtyard outside the club where other people were huddling. They were out of the club, but they had to get away. Rizzo ran down an alley to the street. Others knocked at the homes next to the Grove and begged to be allowed to cut through.

Just before 10:00 p.m., Goody Goodelle was singing her heart out in the Melody Lounge, perched at her piano on the revolving stage. She was wearing one of her favorite outfits, a red velvet dress. She was focused on performing the song "Bell Bottom Trousers" and heard the bartender telling a busboy to put a bulb back into a palm tree where it had been taken out. "Bell bottom trousers, coat of navy blue / She loves her sailor, and he loves her too," she sang. Out of the corner of her eye, she saw the busboy strike a match. Fire then appeared in the fabric cloth that covered the lounge's ceiling. Goody's hands froze on her piano keys as an inner voice said, "Don't panic, don't panic." And then fire was all around. Goody leaped from her piano bench and bolted toward the door to the kitchen, a route she had just recently learned about. She grabbed the hand of a cashier and tried to pull her with her. The woman didn't want to leave her register. "You can come back if they put it out," Goody cried. The pair dashed into the kitchen and told the staff that the lounge was on fire. At first, they thought she was joking. Goody and the cashier ran through the kitchen and up behind the stage. They found a window behind blackout curtains, but it had bars across it. Goody thought she would never get through the narrow bars, but others seemed to be getting out and then so did she, falling on a pile of sand left over from construction of the new lounge. Goody stumbled down an alleyway to the outside of the club; she was not hurt but trying to hold back waves of panic. Clad in only her red velvet dress, Goody was freezing; she found a pay phone to call her mother. Mrs. Maclone had not been listening to the radio, and when her daughter called, the first thing she snapped was, "So, who got shot?" "No, there was a fire. Can you come get me?"

Even as the main dining room was erupting in chaos, drinking continued in the new cocktail lounge that opened on Broadway, often referred to as the Broadway lounge. Mixing drinks was bartender William "Bubbles" Shea, who topped the scales at 385 pounds. Singer Maxine Coleman was performing,

Navy lieutenant junior grade John H. Senft, twenty-nine, of Chicago, was assigned to the Massachusetts Institute of Technology in Cambridge across the Charles River from Boston, where he was in the aeronautical engineering department. Around 9:45 p.m., Senft arrived at the lounge with a few of his fellow officers. The new lounge seemed to be a lovely place—there was a singer and a piano player, officers with their wives and girlfriends and only two drunken men, who apparently had been at the BC–Holy Cross game, wearing some kind of arm bands. Senft heard a strange, somewhat muffled sound, almost like a hiss or rushing water from a pressure discharge. Could someone be starting a motor? The piano player grabbed the mike and started to say, "Everyone keep quiet," when flames shot up behind him. At first, Senft, ever the officer, thought he and his fellow officers could get the crowd out in an orderly way. But the flames were moving too fast. Caught in the crush and enveloped in smoke, his group got down on their knees and crawled out the door. Senft would later tell police that his friends got some hatchets off their truck and tried to break the glass doors to get to people still in the club. "They shouted into the people, and they did get one fellow up on the brick walls and they couldn't get him over—he was too heavy—and the flames enveloped him."

In the new lounge was James Welansky, brother of the club owner, seated at a table with Suffolk County assistant district attorney Garrett Byrne and Boston police night captain Joseph Buccigross. An employee sprinted up to Welansky to tell him that the club was on fire. Barely had the words left her mouth when smoke started to pour into the lounge, followed by a rush of people who had managed to navigate the passageway from the dining room. Buccigross attempted to call for order; he was knocked aside. Somehow, he, Welansky and Byrne managed to reach the doors leading out of the lounge.

They were among the lucky ones. Of the two doors that led into the lounge, the inside vestibule door opened inward, against the flow of human traffic bearing down on it. As people—many rushing in from the main dining area—scrambled to get out, the crowd pushed the inner door shut, and the crush prevented it from opening. Others helplessly beat on the lounge's block glass windows as people collapsed amid the flames and smoke.

Meanwhile, huddled behind the bar in the Melody Lounge, Weiss slowly realized that the fire seemed to be gone. The lounge was totally quiet, although filled with smoke and a strange pungent odor. He rose and, tripping over bodies, stumbled into the kitchen, where, to his astonishment, a group of people remained huddled. Among them was head cashier Katherine Swett, determined not to leave the club's money unguarded. Now certain he knew a way out, Weiss convinced the group to follow him through the basement furnace room to a service door. But the sight of the furnace's lights and heat spooked the group, and they ran back into the kitchen. Weiss tried to argue, but they said they'd stay put and wait for firefighters. Weiss promised to send help and dashed through the furnace room. In the searing heat, he found a service exit and escaped into the cold air. The party he had tried to lead out were later found to have died in the fire, Swett among them. Weiss could do little more than help pull out bodies; he helped bring out more than twenty before he collapsed about 12:30 a.m.

It is difficult to determine why some escaped and some didn't. As in many disasters, memories can be faulty and distorted. Survivors and witnesses told conflicting stories, and those stories often changed over time. Busboy Tony Marra, a fifteen-year-old Everett High School student, had just started

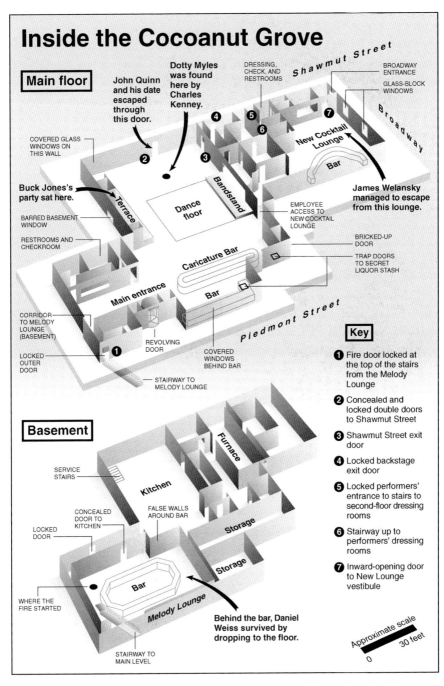

This diagram illustrates the issues with the exits of the club and the location of victims throughout the complex. *Illustration by Jeff Walsh for Commonwealth Editions.*

working weekends at the Grove. He was in the pantry on the dining room floor, where he had been helping with the lights for the show, when he saw smoke. Through the glass window, he could see and hear people running and yelling. He ran down into the kitchen, but the smoke was getting thick and he didn't know what to do. He told police he managed to get out through a window with John Rizzo. That's what he said right after the fire. Beginning about 1962, he told a more elaborate story, including this account to Boston reporter Joe Heaney:

> *I remember running down into the kitchen trying to beat the heat and flames. I stuck my face in front of a fan but it didn't do any good. Everything was still sizzling. Then I stuck my face in an ice cream cooler and smeared maple walnut all over my head. But I was afraid the building would collapse with my hand in the cooler. I crawled on the floor over bodies to three walk-in freezers already crowded with people and tried to get in. I beat on the door but they wouldn't let me in. "Let me in," I cried. "I'm only 15 years old, I don't want to die." "Get out of here kid—there's no more room left." Finally, I crawled on the floor, something my father once taught me. He was an auxiliary firefighter in Everett. Then I grabbed a whiskey bottle, smashed the window and crawled out.*

The streets outside the club were bedlam—a mix of the living and the dead, rescue workers and firefighters. Some who managed to get out walked a few steps and collapsed as the cold air hit their lungs. Victims screamed for help, husbands screamed for wives and friends were frantically searching for friends. When singer Billy Payne got out, "My reaction was to lose everything in my stomach.…I met Mickey Alpert with a woman's white coat on and he hugged me." Among the mass of humanity was Father Maurice Dullea, SJ, performing last rites. As brother Ned Dullea wrote in his diary: "Maurice called from B.C. at 9 A.M., telling me that he had been in the city all night helping to minister to the dead and dying, and searching for Fred Naumetz [the Boston College football co-captain], after a police sergeant had identified one of the dead as Freddie." (Naumetz never went to the club; he had been with friends.)

People coming out of other nightclubs and movie theaters nearby pitched in, including thirty-three-year-old attorney Frank Shapiro. Coming out of the Metropolitan Theatre with his wife, he saw the smoke and heard the fire engines. He sent his wife home and ran over to help, dragging bodies, living and dead, from the club's doors and laying them on the sidewalk. Shapiro later learned a cousin, medical student Joseph Dreyfus, was caught in the fire. A few would-be rescuers tried to get inside the club; among them was Gloucester sailor Stanley Viator, who had been passing through the area when the fire broke out. He repeatedly dashed into the club to pull out patrons. On his fourth trip, he did not come out. The boyfriend of chorus girl Jackie Maver, U.S. Navy seaman Albert Drolette, ran to the Grove when he heard of the fire, not realizing his girlfriend had made it out. He charged into the building only to become trapped inside. He was rescued when someone saw his hand moving in a pile of bodies. He was badly injured but recovered.

Seaman Howard E. Sotherden of Tiverton, Rhode Island, who was in Boston on a two-day pass, heard about the fire and took a taxi to the club to help with rescue efforts. He braved the choking smoke to pull out four people: two dead, two alive. As he pulled out one man whose glasses still hung by one ear, he heard someone say in astonishment, "Hey, that's Marty Sheridan." The half-conscious Sheridan was put in a taxi and taken to Massachusetts General Hospital.

Coast Guardsman Clifford Johnson, who was a patron in the club, was also intent on rescue. The Missouri resident had managed to escape the fire without injury. But he returned time and time again, trying to find his date. On his fourth trip out, he exited in a ball of flames. He was rushed to Boston City Hospital with second- and third-degree burns over 75 percent of his body. Nurses stripping the uniform from his body could not tell where the cloth ended and charred flesh began. The burns were so deep, two of his ribs were exposed, and they could not find an unburned spot on his body to take blood pressure. Although in deep shock, he was alive. The staff knew all they could do would be to ease him into death.

The carnage took a matter of minutes. Aided by a curious coincidence, the main body of the fire was extinguished relatively quickly. When the Melody Lounge was going up in flames, firefighters were only a few blocks away, putting out a minor car fire.

5

FIGHTING THE FIRE

A man came out of the darkness and he was all on fire. These are the things that stick out in your mind....I reached in to take hold of him and...he just puffed right up and I couldn't hold him and he fell back into the fire and then we continued on.
—*Interview with firefighter John "Johnny" Rose by former firefighter and fire historian Charles Kenney, circa November 1991*

A t 10:15 p.m. on November 28, the Boston Fire Department received an alarm from box number 1514 in the theater district; a passerby wanted to report a fire in a parked car near the corner of Stuart and Carver Streets. Because that alarm box was in a high-density area just a few blocks from the Cocoanut Grove and other nightclubs, a contingent of firefighters and apparatus responded, including Engine Companies 7, 10, 22 and 45, Ladder 13 and 17 and Rescue 1. Engine 22, first on the scene, extinguished the car fire within a minute. No one was inside, and likely it was caused by a smoldering cigarette.

Lieutenant Miles Murphy and Charles Kenney of Rescue 1, John "Johnny" Rose of Engine 22, Captain Jeremiah Cronin and George "Red" Graney of Engine 35 and other men used this as a chance to chat. It had been a rough two weeks for the city's firefighters. Thirteen days earlier, in the early hours of November 15, 1942, a fire erupted at the rear of the Luongo Restaurant in the Old Armory Building in Maverick Square, East Boston. East Boston fire companies responded, and just as the fire

For many firefighters, the Cocoanut Grove was a seminal event and a horrific memory. *Courtesy of Boston Public Library.*

appeared to be under control, a wall of the building collapsed, killing six firefighters and injuring forty-three more. It took eighteen hours to retrieve the dead and the injured. The Boston fire service grieved as a family; a loss of one was a loss for all.

Among the firefighters responding to the car fire on November 28 was Charles Kenney, a forty-two-year-old native of Somerville, a husband and father of three children. As his grandson would later write in his family memoir, *Rescue Men*, Kenney "had held many jobs, yet none brought him the satisfaction of firefighting, and he could not imagine retiring. As a firefighter you had the chance to do something that mattered; something that was, in its way, noble. It was a job with a rare purity, a beautifully simple mission: to save lives." Kenney grieved for his fellow firefighters killed and also for those so badly injured they could not stay on the job.

While he loved firefighting, Kenney was aware of the risks he faced every day. Any fire could turn into a life-changing disaster. So he and the other men were relieved that the car fire was so minor. As the men were leisurely putting away their equipment and preparing to return to quarters, they heard a commotion about 10:20 p.m. They first thought a fight—probably between a couple of sailors—had broken out at the nearby Cocoanut Grove. Then, "Hey, there's another fire," someone shouted, and the firefighters could see clouds of smoke billowing from Broadway. Almost at that moment, someone pulled fire alarm box 1521 at 10:20 p.m. at Church and Winchester Streets, and a wife of an off-duty firefighter, who had already rushed downstairs, was telephoning the fire department to report she could see smoke at the Cocoanut Grove from her second-story window.

Members of Engine Company 22 revved their engine and quickly drove down Stuart Street to Broadway. Halting near the corner of Broadway and Shawmut Street, they could see a commotion at the door of the Broadway lounge—it looked like a couple of sailors were fighting. As the men broke away and started running, Johnny Rose could see flames erupting from the doorway. Instinctively, the crew went into action, hooking up their hoses to a hydrant. The flames and the mass exodus blocked the firefighters from getting inside, but the men sent water streaming over the doorway. Rose knew there was a lot of fire inside but had no idea on how many people were involved. Then the exodus seemed to slacken; apparently, people inside were being overcome, burned and trampled. Firefighters from Ladder 13 tried to smash the glass block windows to get to people inside; the modern windows resisted the fiercest blows. When the men finally broke through, they could see burning, blackened hands reaching for help that was coming too late.

Firefighters could not get far inside the door of the Broadway lounge because of the inward-swinging door, which was blocked by fallen bodies. "After ten or fifteen minutes we were still pulling bodies out, passing them behind us and every once in a while, you'd find one that was groaning, but mostly they were burned pretty badly," Rose recalled decades later. It took another half hour to get into the lounge itself. "And still there were people in there at first hollering and screaming, moaning and then there were no moans at all.…We just continued to remove body after body. I never left the Broadway lounge until I was carried out."

As firefighters worked on the Broadway side, Charles Kenney ran to the Shawmut Street door, where flames were shooting out, reaching for oxygen just as the people inside were fighting for their lives. He saw what looked like a growing pile of bodies inside. "Get a line to play in the door,'" Kenney yelled. He didn't want to wait for the water; he wanted to force his way into the building, desperate to get out some of those people. Amid flames and

Firefighters managed with great difficulty to break through the block glass window of the Broadway Lounge to get water on that end of the club. *Courtesy of Boston Public Library Brearley Collection.*

gushing water from hoses, Kenney and other firefighters pulled people and bodies from the club, their hands blackened by heat from the victims' charred flesh. Firefighters smashed the windows on Shawmut and broke through the thin wood panels, trying to vent the fire and provide more exits. Kenney saw, in a pile of bodies, a woman's small hand desperately waving. "Hold on, sister, hold on," he cried and firmly grabbed her wrist, even though he could feel his fingers sinking through burned flesh to bone. "Take it easy. We'll get you out of there in a minute." He could feel her hand grabbing his, grabbing with all her strength. He managed to pull the woman off her feet. Her clothes were torn away, and she was badly burned, but Dotty Myles was carried out alive. Kenney continued to carry out body after body, his lungs bursting from the heat, gas and smoke. He finally collapsed on the street. A sailor and a cab driver got him into a taxi, and he was rushed to Boston City

Hospital. Doctors would later find claw marks on his legs, evidence of the frantic appeals of dying club patrons.

Informed by District Chief Daniel Crowley that people were trapped inside, Deputy Chief Louis Stickel skipped the second alarm and ordered a third; it went out at 10:23. A fourth alarm followed at 10:24 p.m. and a fifth at 11:02 p.m. Eventually, twenty-five Boston engine companies, five ladder companies, one water tower and three rescue companies responded. The firefighters scrambled to send water into the doors and windows on the Shawmut Street side and through the main entrance on Piedmont Street. Aerial ladders went from Shawmut, Piedmont and Broadway, reaching a scared seventeen-year-old dancer named Marshall Cole and other people trapped on the roof. Firefighters jumped on the building to break through the roof, vent the fire and provide access for hoses. An attempt was made to open the rolling roof to vent the blaze, but the firefighters had cut electricity and the roof did not open.

When Engine 35 first pulled up to the club, all Red Graney could see was black smoke. And then he saw a mass of fire and "this fella burning up, all fire, all fire." He managed to get into the club on the Shawmut side, and then he could not move because so many bodies were piled up. "I couldn't go forward, couldn't go to the right but there was a girl on her back," he recalled decades later. She was begging for help, saying her father would be so worried. "I went down to try to help her, and she was pinned...[and then] a big ball of fire came over our heads and I said, 'Holy jumpin' I gotta get some help.' I said, 'I'm coming back.'" He called for another hose line, and firefighters managed to get a charged, high-pressure hose inside. With that water, he pressed forward, allowing others to pull the girl to safety. He was surrounded by piles of bodies.

Meanwhile, fire was shooting twenty feet out from the revolving doors of the main entrance; peering under the arches, firefighters could see the panicked pileup at the revolving door. When they finally smashed through the door, they were driven back by intense heat and flames. All the firefighters could do was pour water into the entryway and watch helplessly as many people burned to death.

Patrick "Joe" Connolly, a tillerman of Ladder 15 and a tough, hefty man, heard the third alarm struck for Box 1521, and as the company rolled, an officer in a passing police car shouted out, "It's the Cocoanut Grove and it's going like hell." The truck took off like a shot. Connolly, who as tillerman controlled the rear, thought he "would fly out of the goddam seat." On arrival, the company was ordered to try to break through the metal door

The fire brought in first responders from all over the city. The police officer on the right was one of three African American officers reported to be at the fire that day. *Courtesy of Boston Public Library.*

on Piedmont that led to the Melody Lounge. "We worked like a sonofabitch with the battering ram, we had to split that door in every direction." Inside was a gruesome sight—there were bodies everywhere, victims of the fruitless effort to get out of the lounge. It was now Connolly's job to remove bodies. "Body after body," he recalled decades later. He ultimately collapsed and regained consciousness in the back of a Boston Protective Company wagon, an oxygen mask on his face and a priest by his side. "Here," said the priest, holding out a pint of whiskey, "Take a slug of this."

"Father, I don't drink."

"Well, you're going to have to take a drink now."

After some argument, Connolly had a gulp; it made him want to throw up, but it brought him back to his senses.

"I'm going back in there—there's too many people there." And he did.

Boston fire chief Samuel J. Pope knew Connolly was a strong, hardened jake and asked him to accompany him to the Melody Lounge. Connolly tried to remove the body of a girl on a piano; she disintegrated in his arms.

He then had to pick up tables and throw them into the corners so bodies could be retrieved. His ladder company worked at the fire for more than five hours. When the engine returned to quarters, only Connolly and the driver were aboard. The rest of the crew had been taken to various hospitals.

The urgent call for help drew U.S. Navy, Army, Coast Guard and National Guard personnel to assist in the evacuation and removal of the injured. So many bodies were being pulled out of the club that rescue workers were forced to make terrible decisions. They would try to determine who was still breathing and get them into transport and pile the corpses like cordwood on the sidewalk. A temporary morgue was established in a nearby garage. A priest moved among the crowd administering last rites. The injured were being hustled into ambulances and any available transportation; police cars, taxis, dump trucks, even passing motorists were being stopped and their vehicles turned into makeshift ambulances. Red Cross chapters from around the area brought in about one thousand volunteers. In the subfreezing temperatures, Red Cross volunteers set up canteens with hot coffee for rescue workers. Boston mayor Maurice Tobin and fire commissioner William Arthur Reilly arrived.

Dotty Myles sat dazed on the sidewalk; apparently, no one thought she would live. Gathering her strength, she leaped into an ambulance that was packed with victims. When it arrived at Boston City Hospital, she was the only one alive.

The eighteen streams of water firefighters poured into the club began to bring the flames under control. When firefighter John Collins pressed into the dining room, the smell of burned flesh was overwhelming. Yet some bodies seemed to be hardly burned at all; there were only slight smudges under their noses. He made his way into the club and down the stairs to the Melody Lounge, where he saw, to his astonishment, a pretty girl sitting at a table with her eyes open and her hand on a cocktail glass. Collins couldn't figure out why she was just sitting here; walking up to her, he realized she was dead.

Among the firefighters was twenty-seven-year-old John F. Crowley of Engine Company No. 9. It was his first shift as a Boston firefighter. As Engine 9 pulled up to the scene, Crowley heard the command, "Run a line from their pump to the doorway on Shawmut Street and get water into the building." As Crowley carried his part of the hose, he passed men and women staggering in a daze, babbling deliriously. He saw others sprawled on the sidewalk, horrifyingly still. Just concentrate on the job, his instincts told him. He and his crew dragged the hose inside the door; bodies were

Despite the horrific loss of life, the fire was extinguished rapidly by firefighters. By 10:45 p.m., the fire was deemed under control. *Courtesy of Boston Public Library.*

piled shoulder high on each side, creating an eerie passageway. As they fumbled in the dark, suddenly the lights came on and the full effect hit Crowley. He saw people still sitting at tables; they had died without even moving. He could see another pile of bodies between the Caricature Bar and what seemed to be a long window. A horrified Crowley realized that the fancy drapery over the window had burned off, revealing light from the lamppost outside; people had seen this light and had thrown themselves over the bar trying to get out. They didn't know that an iron grille covered the outside of the window. They had no chance of escape and died in the smoke and heat.

Although Crowley's company was ready with water, it was not needed. As of 10:45 p.m., the fire was out. The firefighters were now trying to find the living among the dead—a more devastating task than fighting the fire. The "all out" was sounded at 3:42 a.m. As he walked out of the dining room, Crowley saw $1, $2, $5, $10 bills scattered over the floor. How little money meant now, he thought.

6
TREATING THE VICTIMS

When the Cocoanut Grove went up in flames in November 1942 the 171 victims who made it to Boston City and Mass General hospitals alive became subjects in the most comprehensive clinical trial in the annals of burn treatment. The patients exhibited every imaginable burn complication, making it possible to study this most complex of injuries in great detail. New ideas were tried, old methods discarded and the agenda for burn research was set for the next quarter century.
—Burn Unit: Saving Lives After the Flames, *Barbara Ravage, 2004*

B oston City Hospital nurses and doctors were getting a jump on Christmas the night of November 28; many of the staff—even those off-duty—were at the hospital for a holiday party. Most were still celebrating when the first victims of the fire—three men with their hands and face covered with first- and second-degree burns—ran into the hospital. More victims started coming in—by ambulance, private car, taxi and even fire truck. The staff, now realizing a major disaster was in full swing, dived into work; the extra help from partygoers turned out to be a bonus for the terrible nights and days to follow. Soon, a patient was arriving every eleven seconds, which, according to the December 9, 1942 *Boston Traveler*, was "a rate speedier than any ever established by a hospital during London's worst air raids." Of the 311 taken to Boston City Hospital (BCH), 180 were dead on arrival, only 131 would survive the first few hours to be admitted. About 38 more would die within days.

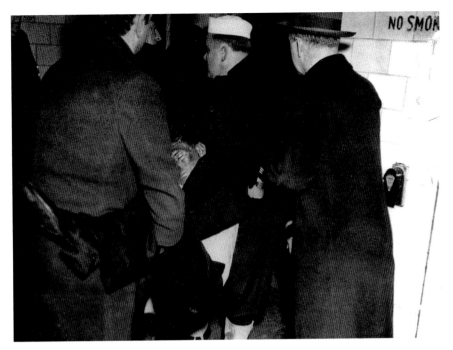

The victims of the Cocoanut Grove presented numerous medical injuries, from severe burns to lung injuries. Some had only smudges of smoke on their faces. *Courtesy of the* Boston Herald.

Doctors and nurses were confronted with a bewildering mix of injuries. Many victims were badly burned, skin curling from their knuckles and arms, their faces already bloating from the terrible heat. Other faces were a deceptively healthy bright red—a sign of carbon monoxide poisoning. Other faces were pale and waxen, the lips blue, an indication that oxygen had been stripped from their blood. Some people were coughing and vomiting black-tinged mucus. Some physicians saw frothy pink secretions on lips—a condition seen on soldiers poisoned by mustard gas in World War I. Some patients walked in on their own, only to collapse before any treatment could be given.

Eerily, some of the dead bore no marks at all, no burns, no discoloration, their eyes closed as if asleep, with only dark smudges under their noses. To Thomas Coleman, a second-year medical student at Massachusetts General Hospital (MGH), the red faces seemed simply to be bright with the "blush of youth." For a fleeting moment, he smelled the fragrance of gardenias—perhaps from corsages. It seemed impossible that these bright souls, silent, still beautiful, would never wake up. "But their flowers aren't burned," he cried. At Boston City Hospital, the staff found, to their horror, one of their own, Gordon Bennet, who had finished his surgical residency less than a month earlier. In a November 30 letter preserved on Digital Commonwealth, BCH surgeon John H.T. McPherson Jr. called Bennet "one of the best loved and most respected people I have ever known." He went on: "The boys on T Surgical—his own service—took care of him. Two special nurses were in constant attendance and seven outside doctors—some of the best in Boston—were on the case but to no avail. He lived 24 hours but never regained consciousness."

Dr. Stanley Levenson, a young burn fellow at Boston City Hospital, had fallen ill from what appeared to be food poisoning after a Thanksgiving meal at the hospital. While still recovering, he received a frantic call from Dr. Charles Lund, BCH head of surgery, and was told that no matter how he felt, he had to report to duty. Choking back nausea from the smell of burned flesh and smoke, Levenson went to work—his first job was to distinguish the living from the dead. He did rounds nonstop twenty-four hours a day for the next three days. An unnamed surgeon wrote that "one case would be rolled out and another in at the same time. Before long all 12 operating rooms were going with everyone working like fury."

At Massachusetts General Hospital, Dr. Francis Moore, a resident on call, listened to a football game and chatted with his colleagues. At about 10:30 p.m., the wails of the first ambulances drifted in above the announcer's voices. Moore paid no attention at first. But the sirens went on and on—Moore donned his white coat and ran toward the emergency room. The full effect of the disaster struck him as he got to the hall outside the ER—the air was rank with the smell of burned clothes and hair, and dead bodies were being lined up in the hall. MGH received 114 patients; within hours, only 39 were alive. As the city's public hospital, Boston City Hospital received far more patients than did MGH.

Contrary to the mythology that injuries were caused by panicked patrons, relatively few patients were suffering from broken limbs caused by the mad panic to exit. MGH staffers found no fractures and only slight trauma to soft parts; William Watters, associate medical examiner for southern Suffolk District, later reported he found only one broken rib. While many patients were obviously injured in the panic, the life-threatening injuries came from the fire and smoke.

By fortunate timing, area hospitals had recently prepared and rehearsed wartime disaster plans in case of an attack on the East Coast. MGH had also conducted two research projects on burn treatment. Now both preparedness and research would be put to the test. Staff administered oxygen, fluids and blood plasma. A nursing supervisor gathered lipsticks from the nurses and used them to mark a large M on the forehead of those who had received morphine. For the next forty-eight hours, nurses and doctors around the city—other Boston-area hospitals also received a smattering of Grove victims—did not sleep.

Their challenges were enormous. Many patients howled with agony or behaved bizarrely—the result of shock and horror. At MGH, Dr. Moore saw a young girl "with her clothing burned off, and her skin hanging like ribbons as she flailed her arms around, screaming with pain. Another, a naval lieutenant who kept repeating over and over again, 'I must find her. I must find her.' His face and hands were the dead paper-white that only a deep third-degree burn can be, and I knew by only looking at him for a moment that if he lived, in two weeks his face would be a red, unrecognizable slough. He didn't live."

Years later, Levenson recalled for a *Boston Globe* article published on May 25, 1992, "We had so little technology. One respirator on each floor at best….We were giving oxygen directly through green rubber tubes."

Boston City Hospital staff struggled to deal with patients stirring restlessly or shaking with chills and nausea. Even those who arrived at the hospital with minimal burns began to have difficulty breathing, their coughing and wheezing becoming severe as their breathing passages were blocked by swelling. "I feel like I'm being choked," many gasped to nurses.

The standard treatment for burns at that time was to remove dead and decaying tissue and blisters from the burned skin (something called debridement) and apply tannic acid to create a leathery scab that would seal the wound and prevent infection. In another recent innovation, burns were sprayed with something called a "triple dye," a mix of textile dyes, or silver nitrate to seal the wound. Dr. Oliver Cope, then a promising researcher at MGH and later president of the American Surgical Association, wanted to try a new approach; he believed body fluid loss and internal infection posed a greater immediate danger than skin damage and thus treatment of shock and other internal problems was initially just as—if not more—important than treating the actual burns. He had been researching a new kind of treatment in which burns were wrapped with a fine mesh gauze impregnated with a petroleum jelly and boric acid mixture and intensive intravenous fluids were administered. Cope and colleague Dr. Bradford Cannon would try the process on a large scale, aided by residents such as Dr. Moore.

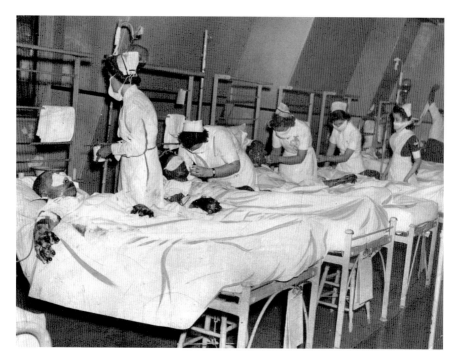

Cocoanut Grove patients treated at Boston City Hospital. *Courtesy of Bill Noonan.*

As burn victims came in, sterile towels were placed over their wounds; when a patient was settled, the burn surfaces were covered with the boric-impregnated gauze. The burns were neither cleansed nor debrided, and the dressings were not changed until the fifth or tenth day. The results, as Cope later put it, were "gratifying." Second-degree wounds healed with minimal scarring; deeper burns were free of invasive infection. Patients were also given blood plasma intravenously to boost blood volume and help prevent shock. At the time, the technology for separating plasma from blood cells and supplying it for injection into the blood was only four years old.

After Cope and Dr. Cannon published their results in the *Annals of Surgery* in 1943, doctors began to change procedures for treating burns, shifting to the "softer" petroleum jelly and boric acid approach. "The advantage lies in its simplicity," as Cope noted.

Even if burns were being successfully treated, patients were in grave danger from infections. Many were given sulfadiazine, a relatively new class of agents aimed at controlling lethal blood infections such as staphylococcus aureus. An urgent request went out for a brand-new substance that seemed miraculous in its ability to halt infection. It was a mold-produced agent and a highly guarded government secret, reserved for the military. Fewer than one hundred people in the United States had been treated with it. It was something called penicillin.

Merk and Company rushed a thirty-two-liter supply of the drug in culture liquid form 368 miles to MGH from New Jersey with a police escort. Even so, the physicians at MGH barely knew how to use the new drug; it was administered topically, not intravenously. Because penicillin was administered in such low doses on Grove patients, its efficacy could not be clearly established. But publicity about this new "miracle" drug convinced the previously skeptical American pharmaceutical industry to start producing mass quantities of the agent. It was the beginning of the age of antibiotics.

Burns, horrible as they were, were overshadowed by respiratory problems. "It was obvious almost at once that we were dealing with something more than the problem of burned skin, a severe impairment of respiration also existed," Cope would write in the *New England Journal of Medicine*. About 107 of the 131 admitted to Boston City Hospital and 36 of the 39 living at MGH suffered some kind of lung damage. Physicians at both hospitals

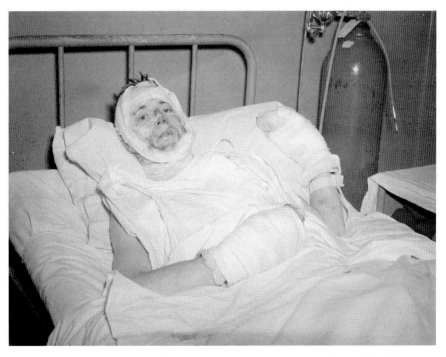

Burn victim from the Cocoanut Grove in hospital bed. *Courtesy of the Boston Public Library, Leslie Jones Collection.*

were puzzled by what had caused such extensive lung injuries, including distinct respiratory lesions. Generally, the more badly burned patients had the most severe lung problems—but a significant minority of patients had severe and even fatal respiratory lesions even if they had minimal or no burns. Dr. Levenson was among the doctors mystified by the wholesale destruction in lower airways below the vocal cords and unusual lesions in the lungs; he initially suspected the fire had released a pulmonary irritant, phosgene, possibly as product of burning freon, a common refrigerant coolant. Other experts and witnesses insisted the nightclub smoke wasn't just ordinary smoke.

"Many of the victims had the appearance of soldiers I saw gassed in the first world war," William J. Brickley, medical examiner for Northern Suffolk County, testified in hearings after the fire. Medical examiner Timothy Leary of Southern Suffolk testified, "There is no question, however, but that there was something poisonous beside carbon monoxide in that smoke." Newspapers buzzed with speculation about the "mystery gas," but the exact properties could not be determined.

The "mystery gas" puzzled Boston for months. Dr. Levenson later concluded that the severe lung damage was caused not by phosgene but by the chemicals in smoke, ranging from carbon monoxide to hydrogen cyanide, ordinarily produced when wood, paper and textiles were partially burned. Those who covered their faces with a damp cloth—like bartender Daniel Weiss—managed to escape with little damage. Those who passed out and continued to breathe smoke suffered the worst damage. Three years after the fire, Harvard Medical School researchers found that when the leatherette that covered the club's wall and furniture was subjected to extreme heat, it produced the potentially lethal fume acrolein, a substance found in tear gas. Acrolein was suggested as the "mystery gas" that caused lesions in the victims' lungs.

In 1992, Jeffrey R. Saffle, MD, FACS, wrote in the *American Journal of Surgery*:

> *Fifty years after the Cocoanut Grove Fire, we can now appreciate that physicians at both hospitals were describing that for the first time in a systematic manner, the effects of inhalation injury. There was no mysterious "poison gas" at the Cocoanut Grove, merely smoke itself, which proved to be poisonous enough. Smoke from the combustion of wood, paper or plastic is now known to contain a host of respiratory toxins.*

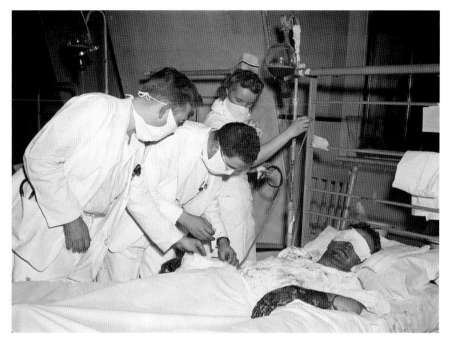

Cocoanut Grove burn victim receiving blood plasma. *Courtesy of the Boston Public Library, Leslie Jones Collection.*

The trauma for the area's medical and nursing staff would go on for weeks as patients succumbed to injuries. Of three BCH patients with burns over 30 percent of their body, one died in four hours, one in twenty-eight days and another nearly six months later. In the critical need for blood, hospital staff lined up to donate. Others stood outside on the street, pulling in passersby on foot and in cars, begging for help. Bostonians responded: 1,200 citizens gave blood within days.

The fire brought together the city's medical staff, as all were in a battlefield together. Every life was precious, and everything would be done to save as many as possible. Boston City Hospital would assume medical costs, supplemented by the Red Cross. Levenson told the *Globe*, "We had great attending doctors, residents, medical students and most of all we had wonderful nurses."

Hospital nurses were a key group of medical professionals deeply affected by the fire and often overlooked in accounts of the disaster. They provided round-the-clock, hands-on bedside care for patients, attending to both physical and emotional needs. They handled the delicate job of debriding, done with instruments and without the rubber gloves that are used today. For many nurses, the Cocoanut Grove was a life-changing experience on both a personal and professional level. Barbara Poremba, EdD, MPH, RNCS, ANP, professor emeritus at Salem State University, has been conducting ongoing research of nurses and the Cocoanut Grove fire, and she shared some of her published material with me in an interview by Zoom and by correspondence.

Poremba interviewed Anne Montgomery Hargreaves, MS, RN, FAAN, who was a student nurse at Boston City Hospital in 1942. She and other student nurses were enjoying the hospital's holiday party when a supervisor interrupted the festivities to tell them they were to quickly put on their uniforms and immediately report to the unit they had been assigned that day. Hargreaves went to the "Accident Department"—which was then the term for the emergency department because it consisted only of a few rooms designated for broken bones and stitches, not suites set up for trauma teams, with technology and equipment as today. Instead, patients would be sent directly to wards. She was assigned to guard a small room at the end of the corridor being used as the temporary morgue and told to make sure that no one stole any valuables from the victims. This was a crucial job—bodies were badly burned, and many women were separated from their purses, so jewelry and other personal objects would be vital in identification. But it was a frightening experience for the young woman as she witnessed the mayhem of critically injured and dead carried into the hospital with great speed. When she finally made her way home on a streetcar the next morning, she was conscious that she smelled horribly and thought all the passengers were looking at her, even though they said nothing. She would later tell Poremba, "I was wondering, what have I gotten myself into? I'm just a kid, what am I doing?" She arrived home, cleaned herself up, slept and went back the next day, the smell lingering for days. In the weeks ahead, she helped care for many seriously burned victims.

Due to the shortage of nurses because of the war, young nurses were thrust into positions that would tax even the most senior professionals. Helen Berman Abramson, MSN, RN, had been working at Boston City Hospital for only three months while awaiting deployment to the Army Air Corps. She was assigned night supervisor of the neuro operating room because, as she told Poremba years later, "I was the supervisor because I was the only nurse there." She rushed to bring bandages and IVs to different parts of the ward. She described the scene to Poremba as "bedlam." Victims were just "pouring in so fast that if they fell off of the stretcher, they just left them there." Many were already dead, and those still alive were in agony from burn injuries. Some were just in shock. "We didn't have time to ask for names. We just medicated everyone with morphine as fast as we could, using our red lipstick to mark 'M' on their forehead." When Poremba asked Abramson what she was thinking at the time, she quickly replied, "You didn't think, you just did."

Nurses played a huge role in the treatment of Clifford Johnson, the twenty-year-old Coast Guardsman who had so bravely tried to rescue people from the fire. Against all expectations, he survived the night at Boston City Hospital. His back, buttocks and legs "were not just burned, they were charred," as author Paul Benzaquin later wrote in a 1959 article in *Life* magazine. The ends of two ribs were exposed. Burns on his chin exposed the jawbone. "Rarely had anyone ever survived with a third of [their] skin burned away. Johnson had lost more than half of his," Benzaquin wrote.

Among his nurses was Mary Creagh, a native of Ennis, County Clare, Ireland. She and other nurses spent hours with Johnson, administering medications and blood transfusions, cleaning wounds and changing difficult dressings using instruments in place of sterile gloves, monitoring vital signs, preparing and providing pureed food and fluids through a stomach tube, performing physical and respiratory therapy and caring for all of his bodily needs. They comforted him, as he was often in delirium or terrible pain. No one thought that he would live, but with his round-the-clock care, he clung to life. Creagh never forgot him or the horrors she saw. She often awoke screaming from flashbacks of seeing so many bodies still dressed in their evening finery laid out in the BCH parking lot. Her son Kenneth Marshall, who became a physician, was also profoundly affected by his mother's experience (see chapter 11).

According to Poremba, nurses were able to learn so much about burn treatment that Massachusetts General Hospital sent nurses to assist in the care of the burn victims of the Hartford Circus Fire in July 1944. While the Cocoanut Grove fire produced a large number of innovations in burn and lung treatment, "really, it was because of the compassionate care that was given by the skilled nurses that made those treatments successful and that impacted the survival of these victims," Poremba said. "Without that nursing care, they would not have survived."

The injuries of the Cocoanut Grove fire went deeper than the skin and lungs in ways that medical professionals were just beginning to understand.

A young girl of sixteen was brought into the hospital with severe burns and lung injuries. The hospital staff learned that she had lost both her parents and her boyfriend in the fire—her boyfriend's father was also killed

PAGE SIX   THE BOSTON HERALD, MC

4 Members Of 2 Keene Families Die

2 Others Injured in Fire at Party Given Fred Sharky's Sons

KEENE, N. H., Nov. 29—A night club party arranged for two high school students as a finale to attendance at the B. C.-Holy Cross football game in Boston, wounded up in death in the Cocoanut Grove fire for four members of two Keene families and serious injury to two others.

Killed were:

Fred P. Sharby, 42, and his son, Fred, Jr., 19, of 240 Roxbury street, and Clyde C. Clark, 39, and his wife, Mabel, 40, of 171 Court street, Keene.

Injured and in Massachusetts General Hospital are:

Mrs. Sharby and Ann Marie Clark, 16, daughter of the ill-fated couple.

It was a gay party the Sharbys and Clarks were having. In the afternoon they had been to the football game at Fenway Park. It was the first big college game that Fred and Marie had ever seen. Then it was decided to attend a night club, likewise the first time the two youngsters had ever been to one.

A seventh member of the party escaped death or injury by leaving the night club early to go to the Hotel Statler with friends. She is Pauline Sharby, 21, a Regis College student. On learning of the fire, Pauline called her home in Keene, received no answer and walked streets in the fire district in frantic inquiry for her family. She did not learn of the tragedies until friends from Keene, who came to Boston to make identifications, found her.

The entire day—the game and night club—had been arranged for the Sharby boy, who had been a backfield star on the Keene high school eleven, and for Ann Marie,

FAMILY TRAGEDY—Anna Marine Clark, 19, left, is in a serious condition at Massachusetts General Hospital as a result of injuries received in the Cocoanut Grove fire which cost the lives of her mother, Mrs. Mabel Bushaw Clark, center, and her father, Clyde C. Clark, right, 39-year-old manager of the F. M. Johnson Lumber Company, Keene, N. H.

FATHER AND SON DEAD—Fred P. Sharby, 42, center, former official of the Keene, N. H. lodge of Elks and his 19-year-old son, Fred P. Sharby, Jr., lost their lives and Mrs. Sharby, right, was badly injured in Saturday night's disaster.

Newspaper clipping of Ann Clark and family. *Photo by author.*

and his mother injured. Yet during her initial stay in the hospital, the girl showed a kind of cheerful acceptance of the situation. She was discharged in three weeks; she talked rapidly and cheerfully about returning to care for her siblings. Over the next two months, she continued to recover, and her sisters were placed in other homes. At the end of ten weeks, she entered a true state of grief. She became depressed, with frequent crying and a feeling of emptiness in her body and tightness in her lungs. She became vividly preoccupied with her deceased parents. The adults around her may have felt she was lucky to have survived the fire, but she didn't feel lucky. She felt that her world was collapsing.

That girl was Ann Marie Clark, the sixteen-year-old mentioned in chapter 3, who was dancing in her boyfriend's arms when the fire broke out. She had lost both parents, Clyde and Mabel Clark; her boyfriend, Fred Sharby Jr.; and her boyfriend's father, Fred Sharby, in the fire. Her older sister, Pauline, age twenty-one, a Regis College student, had been with the party at the club but left to go to be with friends at the Statler Hotel. Pauline and Ann's younger sister were all that was left of her family. And while she initially seemed to be recovering from her losses and her wounds, the damage went far deeper. Her case caught the attention of a psychiatrist who was beginning to study the lingering effects of grief and trauma.

Dr. Erich Lindemann moved to the United States from his native Germany in 1929 to conduct psychology research at the University of Iowa. He came to Harvard on a research fellowship and later became the chief of a psychiatric outpatient department at Massachusetts General Hospital. The mental anguish of Cocoanut Grove survivors now triggered his intense interest.

He observed a man whose daughter died in the fire: the father kept picturing her calling his name from a telephone booth. The sound became so loud and the scene so vivid that he often forgot his immediate surroundings. Other survivors, even though they recovered from their injuries, barely had enough energy to climb a staircase. Food tasted like sand. Nothing seemed worth living for.

In a landmark paper coauthored with Stanley Cobb, "Symptomatology and Management of Acute Grief," published in the *American Journal of Psychiatry* in 1944, Lindemann used the example of Cocoanut Grove patients and other patients to note, "Acute grief is a definite syndrome with psychological and somatic symptomatology....The bereaved searches the time before the death [of a loved one] for evidence of failure to do right by the lost one." Today we might define this as post-traumatic stress disorder.

He described in detail the case of a thirty-two-year-old man who received only minor burns in the fire. When he learned after five days that his wife, Grace, had died in the nightclub fire, he seemed somewhat relieved he did not have to worry about her fate. On January 1, however, his family returned him to the hospital because he had become restless, agitated, even frightened, and unable to concentrate on any organized activity. He remained preoccupied and agitated at the hospital. "He would try to read, drop it after a few minutes, or try to play ping pong and give it up after a short time. He would try to start conversations, break them off abruptly, and then fall into repeated murmured utterances: 'Nobody can help me. When is it going to happen? I am doomed, am I not?' His morbid feelings of guilt made him relive the fire—how he was trying to pull his wife out when he fainted. He should have been able to save her, or he should have died too. After four days, he became calmer and seemed to be gaining control of himself." On the sixth day, "after skillfully distracting the attention of his special nurse, he jumped through a closed window to a violent death."

The name of that thirty-two-year-old, Francis Gatturna, is now included with that of his wife as a victim of the fire.

Gatturna's mental trauma was not unique; other fire victims reported getting panic attacks in restaurants. Those more severely burned felt disfigured, with no chance at future happiness. "It seems that the grieving person can delay his grieving period but not avoid it and that individuals who show no signs of grief during the period of convalescence from their somatic injuries are likely to have disabling disturbances at a later period," Lindemann concluded. In 1948, he helped found Human Relations Service in Wellesley Hills, the first community mental health agency in the nation.

For many in Boston, grieving over the Cocoanut Grove fire would go on for years, often without closure or resolution.

7

AS THE ASHES COOLED

My father's sister was the youngest victim of the Cocoanut Grove fire.
She was 15 years old. She died at [the club] *where she did not want to attend.*
She was almost forced into going to the Cocoanut Grove with her brother, who
just returned back from the war. She pleaded with her mother and father not to go.
She died in the fire along with my uncle's wife. [My family] *blamed each other.*
They all went to the grave blaming one another for making Eleanor
go to the Cocoanut Grove.
—*David Chiampa, interview with author, December 9, 2010,*
in Quincy, Massachusetts

The headlines of Boston newspapers on November 29 and thereafter screamed with horror and confusion: "400 Dead in Hub Night Club Fire, Hundreds Hurt in Panic as Cocoanut Grove Becomes Wild Inferno," the *Boston Globe* declared. Cried the *Herald*: "450 Die as Flames and Panic Trap Cocoanut Grove Crowd, Scores of Service Men Are Lost, Fire Worst in City's History, Few Victims Identified." The *Boston Advertiser*: "399 Dead, 200 Injured in Cocoanut Grove Fire: Scores Held in Trap by Wild Panic."

Among the list of the dead on the front page of the *Boston Globe* were the names of Mr. and Mrs. Martin Sheridan. But Marty was very much alive. In fact, the Nazis had captured him. As he drifted in and out of consciousness, he knew that agents of the Third Reich were taking blood for experimentation. That's why he couldn't see anything—his face and hands

A headline in the *Boston Advertiser* on November 29, 1942.

were wrapped in bandages. But he could sense people bustling around him, using words like *edema* and *intravenous*. "You can't fool me with those medical terms," he whispered weakly as he drifted back to sleep.

Hours later, when he began to gain consciousness, he recognized the voice of a friend, a doctor. He began to remember being at the Cocoanut Grove and weakly mouthed questions like, "Where is my wife?" "Everything is going to be all right," the doctor said nervously and excused himself. Only after a few days did Sheridan's father gently tell him that his wife, Connie, never made it out alive and most of the party of movie executives and their wives were dead. Sheridan, in agony with his burns, could barely comprehend what had happened. And where was Buck Jones?

The losses piled up, the stuff of nightmares, of terrible ironies and tragic coincidences.

Dead were the newlyweds John and Claudia Nadeau O'Neil with their best man, John F. Doyle, and the maid of honor, who was the groom's sister, Anna O'Neil. They were never to see the photo snapped by Grove photographer Lynn Andrews of their smiling faces. Their marriage had lasted three hours.

Four sons of a seventy-one-year-old widow, Mary Fitzgerald of Wilmington, Massachusetts, were dead. James, John, Henry and Wilfred were at the club to fete Henry Fitzgerald, age twenty-eight, a private first class in the Army Air Corps, home on a furlough. Their mother learned of their deaths in an agonizing series of calls, one after the other. "It can't be true my fine boys are dead, they went away so happy, so glad to be with each other and to give Henry a real welcome," she cried to a *Boston Globe* reporter. The brothers would be buried side by side.

A party composed mostly of members of the Whitmarsh family died in the fire. The three young Whitmarsh children lost their father, mother, grandfather, grandmother and two aunts. Dozens of children lost both their parents.

About sixty-four U.S. military personnel, including two WAVEs, were dead. Two passing rescue workers died: Harold Hawkins, age forty-six, of Boston, an assistant steward at the nearby Hotel Statler, and Seaman Stanley Viator, age twenty-five, U.S. Naval Reserve, Gloucester, Massachusetts. The fire claimed victims from twenty-three different states, plus the District of Columbia and one foreign country. Forty-six teenagers were killed. The youngest victim of the fire was fifteen-year-old Eleanor Chiampa of Newton, Massachusetts, who was at the club with her brother, Lieutenant Benjamin L. Chiampa, and his wife, Giovanna M. "Jennie" Chiampa, and other friends. She was dancing with her brother when the fire broke out; some reports indicated that she escaped the building, but she died three days later. Her brother survived with injuries; his wife died. Eleanor had not wanted to go to the club that night, but her family insisted.

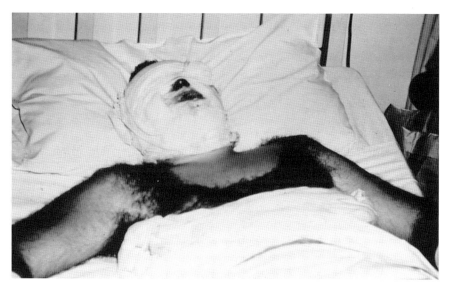

The *Boston Globe* actually listed Martin Sheridan among the dead, but he survived the fire. He was badly burned and required numerous skin grafts. *Courtesy of Martin Sheridan.*

Families sought answers at the morgue about the fate of loved ones. *Courtesy of Boston Public Library.*

Of the party of twenty-nine who accompanied Buck Jones, more than half were dead, including Edward and Beatrice Ansin. Scott Dunlap, Jones's managing agent, producer and friend, survived. Buck Jones was rushed to Massachusetts General Hospital. Dr. Thomas Risley, a surgical intern at MGH, was assigned to treat him. Jones was suffering from both burns and lung injuries. As the cowboy's neck swelled, his breathing tube was blocked, and Risley and another resident spent more than two hours trying to locate his trachea for a tracheotomy. After forty-eight hours, the tough hombre—who survived celluloid gunfights, fisticuffs, chases on horseback and vengeful bad guys—rode off into the sunset. His beloved wife, Odille, and his daughter were racing from California to be by his side. They were halfway across the country when they received the news that he had died.

Buck Jones's Junior Commandos, some of whom had actually just met their hero, were heartbroken. "There were solemn little services of about 3 minutes each held in attics, cellars, barns, churches, schools, front verandas, huts and rooms in the family home. Hymns rolled out of trembling throats and sad hearts" wrote Paul Waitt, the area commando-in-chief, in the December 4 *Boston Traveler*. "I vividly recall the morning of December 1 when as a small boy in England, I listened to the BBC morning news show and was horrified to hear that Buck Jones was dead," Joseph G. Rosa wrote in his 1966 tribute to Jones in *True West* magazine. "At the moment something of my boyhood also died."

True West magazine quoted Hollywood correspondent W.H. Mooring as saying "I dare bet Buck Jones didn't go to a nightclub once in five years. Odd he should have made his last roundup among all the tinsel of city night life. He belongs so completely to the orange grove, the nearby corral and the horses."

On December 7, scores of film notables and "the homespun neighbors who called him pal" paid tribute to Buck Jones in a ceremony in Hollywood. Cowboy friends and actors sang his cowboy songs like "Empty Saddle" and "Home on the Range." His daughter placed a wreath of roses on his coffin with the inscription: "My Buddy." Trem Carr, vice president of Monogram Pictures, reported that he had learned that Jones twice ran back in the club to rescue victims. On his third trip back, he collapsed. This is patently untrue. Yet to her dying day, his widow, Odille, clung to this belief, incredulous that her beloved husband who won the West would be felled without a fight. He died a hero, she was sure. A touching and perhaps more truthful tribute came from Dorothy Wayman in the *Boston Globe*, who described Jones's trip to Children's Hospital in Boston when he delighted a pain-wracked little boy recovering from a mysterious disease who could not yet walk or use his hands. Jones, "just before he went to the Cocoanut Grove dinner party to die, wiped from a child's mind the recollection of past pain and gave him the courage and the 'spunk' to start using the muscles and nerves that the doctors and nurses had cured of disease." Buck Jones's remains were cremated and spread in the ocean off the California coast.

A special section of the December 6, 1942 *Boston Sunday Advertiser* printed the photos and names of victims of the fire—four full pages in all. Both the dead and injured were included.

A special section of the December 6, 1942 *Boston Sunday Advertiser* printed the photos and names of victims of the fire—four full pages in all. Both the dead and injured were included.

A special section of the December 6, 1942 *Boston Sunday Advertiser* printed the photos and names of victims of the fire—four full pages in all. Both the dead and injured were included.

A special section of the December 6, 1942 *Boston Sunday Advertiser* printed the photos and names of victims of the fire—four full pages in all. Both the dead and injured were included.

In early 1943, a Buck Jones War Bond Drive was launched. Western star William Boyd, best known for his role as Hopalong Cassidy, bought a $10,000 bond in his friend's memory. Throughout 1943, newspaper movie ads declared it was "your last chance to see your old time favorite western star Buck Jones in 'Arizona Bound.'" Odille "Dell" Osborne Jones died on April 16, 1996.

The family of twenty-three-year-old Mario David Capone wanted to spare the young soldier from grief, as he was fighting with the U.S. Army in North Africa. They did not tell him that his brother, Charles Capone, had been at the Cocoanut Grove with two friends, John DeMatteo (also their cousin) and Francis Connell. Connell was preparing to ship out, so Charles and John decided they had to take him out for a night on the town, even though the twenty-five-year-old Charles wore a walking cast from an injury. They did not make it out of the club. The grief-stricken Capone family, which ran a road construction company in Dedham, mourned Charles in a December 2 service at the Holy Name Church in West Roxbury at 10:00 a.m.; funeral services had been held at the same church at 9:00 a.m. for Francis Connell.

Mario David Capone had no idea of the tragedy until January 5, when he received a sympathy letter from a friend for the death of his brother. He was distraught, writing in his journal, "I hope now, I never get home." Even in a war zone, he was shocked by the news. He had a mass said for his brother on January 17 at a Catholic church in Casablanca. "I am worrying myself to death about how the folks are taking it and all. Also, how Charlie had to die at such a young age. He was one swell fellow and I shall never forget his kindness," he wrote in his journal.

The nightclub's staff was decimated. Katherine Swett, who refused to leave her post, died trying to protect the untouched cash box. Headwaiter Frank Balzarini, who tried to direct patrons out of the club, was dead. The singer Grace McDermott was dead; reportedly, she calmly told James Welansky that the club was on fire and patrons should leave, then dutifully returned to her piano. Maxine Coleman, a beloved, buxom, rowdy singer, was also dead. Broadway lounge bartender Bubbles Shea fought for his life. He had seen dark gray fumes rush into the lounge, and after inhaling the "strong and bitter smoke," he covered his face with a wet bar rag. As he struggled to the exit, he was tripped by the stampede, falling face-down. His clothes caught fire, and his back and shoulders burned—more than 30 percent of his body. BCH staff attempted to save him by immobilizing his burned body face-down. He pleaded with doctors to turn him over. "Please get me off my stomach," he cried repeatedly, as nurses tried to gently explain he needed to stay in that position. After twelve weeks of agony, Shea succumbed. Club cigarette girl Shirley "Bunny" Leslie, age twenty, had been burned out of her home with her mother just two weeks earlier. She died in the fire. Bartender John Brady and busboy Stanley Tomaszewki survived and had done their best to get people to safety. But Stanley was frantic. He could not find his friend Joseph Tranfaglia. He went to Joseph's home, but he was not there. He then went to police to see if he could find out anything, and officers wanted to talk to him. He would later find out his friend was dead.

Jack Lesberg found himself regaining consciousness in Boston City Hospital. Dawn had not yet arrived, but he could feel the pandemonium everywhere. He realized a nearby priest was preparing to give him last rites; "Just a minute," he croaked, as he struggled to open his eyes. A doctor grabbed the priest, and they moved to someone else. Bandleader Bernie Fazioli was rescued along with Lesberg and interviewed by police before he died of his injuries. Saxophonist Romeo Ferrara (who saw himself erroneously listed as dead) and drummer Al Maglitta survived. Al Willet was nowhere to be found. His girlfriend, Henrietta "Pepper" Russell, a dancer who escaped with fellow dancer Jackie Maver, searched for him through the night he was in the hospital—perhaps he had gone home. As morning approached, she forced herself to go to the Southern Mortuary. As a priest tried to comfort her there, they heard a groan from a "body." It was Al. He had been mistakenly transported among the corpses to the mortuary. He would survive.

An aspect of this fire worth noting is the lack of victims of color. This was not a coincidence. A headline in the *Detroit Tribune* of December 12, 1942, spelled it out: "Color Bar Saves Lives of Negroes in Boston's Tragic Cocoanut Grove Fire." The first paragraph reads: "As a result of the omnipresent color bar, the colored section of this town was least affected by the nation's worst holocaust since the General Slocum fire which took 1021 lives in 1904." (The *General Slocum* was a passenger ship that caught fire with about 1,300 passengers on board.) Only one African American died in the fire, Shadrack E. "Shady" Plenty, fifty-five, who was an attendant in the men's bathroom. He was only there filling in for someone on vacation. Usually, he worked at James Welansky's bar. His older sister Maybelle P. Cotton also worked at the club as a ladies' room attendant. She escaped without injury and survived until 1959. Vera B. Daniels, the Black coat room attendant, was rushed with severe injuries to Boston City Hospital, where she was put in a bed in the aisle, as there was no other

A delivery of caskets to the morgue. *Courtesy of Boston Public Library.*

room. According to a Red Cross report, she "prays earnestly to be allowed to live for her child's sake [and] has put up a courageous fight." She would be hospitalized for the next seven months but recovered.

Death notices and funerals filled entire pages of the *Herald* and *Record American*. On December 3 alone, 150 funerals were scheduled. With 19 burials scheduled, the chapel bell tolled almost continuously at the Holy Cross cemetery in Malden. Members of the Boston College football team and the college faculty attended a solemn high requiem mass for four people, including Larry Kenney of Dorchester, who in the role of athletic equipment manager at BC, handed out helmets and towels to Eagle athletes for more than a decade.

A large congregation attended the funeral of fire victim Mary E. "Mae" McCormack, the young daughter of Mr. and Mrs. Edward Joseph "Knocko" McCormack and niece of Congressman John W. McCormack. Her father, known as Knocko from his earlier days as a prizefighter, "was a bootlegger, he was a leg breaker—any time you needed a nasty deed done, you called on Knocko McCormack," as Garrison Nelson, a biographer of John W.

McCormack, told WBUR radio in 2017. The mourners at this daughter's funeral brought prominent politicians, including Mayor Maurice Tobin. The McCormacks were one of Boston's most politically influential families. Knocko was convinced that there had been "payoffs by the nightclub's owner to corrupt city building inspectors," Nelson wrote in his biography of John W. McCormack. When the mayor attempted to console McCormack at the wake, Knocko, a three-hundred-pound bruiser, "brushed aside Tobin's hand and sent a sledgehammer fist into his face," Nelson writes. Whether this story is true or not, fire historian Charles C. Kenney recounted the tale to this author with great glee; this was evidence to him that the failures of the Cocoanut Grove were part of a citywide custom of looking the other way when profits were at stake. And Knocko would know this.

The death and injury toll would not be established for weeks; indeed, in many ways, it has never been sorted out. Estimates ranged wildly in the days after the fire and through the weeks to come as bodies were counted and re-counted and the injured died of their wounds. The identification

The exterior of the Broadway lounge of the Cocoanut Grove after the fire. *Army Signal Corps/Courtesy of Boston Public Library.*

of the badly burned dead presented particular trauma for families and friends; news photos captured the grim stoicism of mothers and fathers lined up outside mortuaries or waiting in the facility's amphitheater—some holding out hope that they would not find a loved face among the charred bodies. Many bodies were burned beyond recognition and required dental records for identification. About 200 people died trying to escape through the revolving doors; another 100 died in the Broadway lounge; a stack of bodies—at least 25 to 30—was found piled behind the bolted exit door from the Melody Lounge on Piedmont Street. Other bodies were found throughout the dining room and Caricature Bar and in the basement. Many victims were found on the raised terrace, which may have been subjected to greater heat. In an official list of victims, the count was put at 490. Published reports, however, often cite 491 or 492 (as this author did). About 166 people were hospitalized from their injuries, and many others who were hurt did not seek medical attention.

One researcher has invested considerable time to come up with a definitive number of dead or, if not, as close to it as we can get. I met David Blaney sometime after I wrote my 2005 book and found out he was meticulously and thoroughly researching the number of those killed and injured in the fire

The wreck of the club from Shawmut Street side. *Courtesy of Boston Public Library.*

and their life stories. Blaney, a Boston-area retail expert, became intrigued with the Grove fire after first starting to look into the 2003 Station Nightclub fire of Rhode Island, which has eerie parallels to the 1942 tragedy. The Grove fire pulled him in—as it has for so many of us in Boston. He has spent years carefully and thoroughly trying to correctly identify each fire victim. He told me, "I love finding new information and I started to focus as time went by less on the story of the fire itself and more on the individuals. It became a challenge. Can I find out what happened to this person? Can I get a picture?" We discussed the final victim count in April and May 2022, as I sought out his help for this edition.

His conclusion: 490 deaths. This includes the tragic suicide of F. Gattura (see chapter 6) and that of Phyllis Atkins, age twenty-two, who died on May 5, 1943, the last official fatality. Blaney carefully went through the records and found several victims who appeared in duplicate form on earlier versions of compiled death lists. He found that victims Mary DeMoura and Mary Travers of Dorchester were the same person. According to Blaney, victim William Meserve was the lone fire victim completely omitted from the final published version.

"I figure if I can do one thing, if I can get the number 490 out there and have people understand that," Blaney said. "I know that's an impossible task because the other numbers have been misreported so often that they're going to be used as sources for years. But I wanted to try to get the facts straight."

Complicating matters a bit, Helen Gross of Brookline, who was badly burned in the fire, died in 1945; her immediate cause of death was breast cancer that had spread to her brain. After much thought, Blaney concluded she probably should not be counted as a victim. "The deciding factor for me was the decision of the attending medical examiner (who had processed dozens of Grove death certificates two years earlier) to classify her death under 'natural causes' rather than accidental," he said.

Correct figures like 490 dead and 166 injured are important, but they can be mind-numbing. Numbers can obscure the sense of individual loss, of trauma that can go on for generations. After this author gave a talk on the fire in Groton, Massachusetts, I was approached by Joseph Short. His uncle was the grandfather of Joseph Tranfaglia, the sixteen-year-old bus boy who died in the fire and who got a job at the Grove for Stanley Tomaszewski. Short showed me Tranfaglia's worn leather wallet. It contained a ticket, a calendar, a poem typed on yellowing paper and one dollar. I asked how he came by the wallet. "It's been handed down through the family. My grandparents had it after he passed away. And it

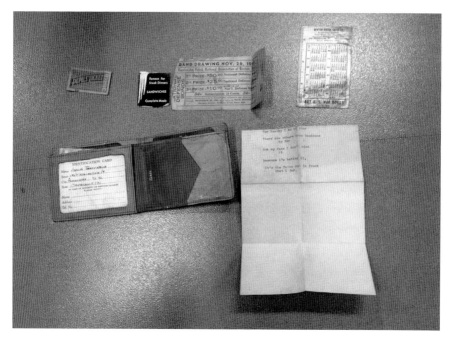

The author has been approached by many people with stories about the fire. In Groton, Joseph Short showed a wallet and its contents that belonged to his relative Joseph Tranfaglia, who died in the fire. There was one dollar in the wallet. The wallet has been handed down through the family. Short said he was named for Tranfaglia. *Photo by author.*

was given to my mother who passed it on to me. I'm named after him.… I've heard nothing but wonderful things about him. All of the sympathy cards speak of him glowingly and I want to know more who [he] was. I knew his sister. I know both his brothers, my uncles, and my mom and my grandparents. I just don't know him."

At another appearance in 2010 in Quincy I spoke to Ina Cutler. She told me, "When I was a young girl living in Plymouth with my family, my mother [Jeanette Zall] was visiting her sister [Ethel Slate] in Quincy. Her sister took her out for a good time. She'd never been in a nightclub before, and we knew nothing about it. But the next morning at about five in the morning, my father got a call saying that there had been a fire." All that day Ina listened to the radio, hearing names of victims. At ten o'clock that night, her father came back from the morgue, and she learned that her mother and aunt had died at the Cocoanut Grove and her uncle was at the hospital. Ethel's husband, Jacob Slate, a tobacco merchant, survived, but he couldn't see and could barely breathe. He was revived with oxygen, but his throat was parched and too dry to swallow.

According to an account by Paul Benzaquin, he begged for olive oil and basted his throat with his fingers until the painful dryness subsided. He would regain his sight and recover.

Young Ina Cutler had to grow up without her mother. "I was the oldest in the family. My sister was six, and we had a baby and my grandmother was staying with us. It was during the war, very difficult to get help. We had a series of housekeepers, and we just sort of pulled ourselves up. Did it affect me? I think it made me a stronger person."

Despite calls to come forward, the man who unscrewed the light bulb never admitted to his action, nor was he ever identified as being among the dead.

8

THE INVESTIGATION AND TRIAL

The hearings of the Fire Commissioner revealed just how the Grove functioned.
Get a politician to use pressure on officials, pack in as many people as you can
and do things as cheap as possible.
—*Boston District fire chief John Vahey in "Design for Disaster," a report on the*
fire published by the Boston Sparks Association in 1970

Immediately after the fire, in a classic case of closing the barn door
après cattle departure, Boston officials suspended the entertainment
permits of 35 hotels and 682 restaurants and taverns. An investigation
was launched—in fact, several investigations were launched. The next
day, Boston Police began interviewing witnesses, and Fire Commissioner
William Arthur Reilly opened up a special investigation. Under some
pressure, these hearings were open to the press. It wasn't until 2012 that
the witness transcripts from the Boston Police Department were released
to the public and posted online, and those statements provide additional,
if sometimes conflicting, details on what people saw, heard and smelled in
the moments after the fire began.

By contrast, the Reilly hearings were breathlessly covered by the press.
The hearings started the Sunday after the fire and ended on January
20, 1943. There were more than two hundred witnesses, and over one
thousand pages of testimony were produced. What is remarkable is despite
this vast amount of material, so much about the Cocoanut Grove fire and
its operations still remained murky.

Stanley Tomaszewski was the sixteen-year-old busboy who lit a match to find a way to put in a lightbulb in a palm tree in the downstairs Melody Lounge. *Courtesy of Boston Public Library.*

There are, for example, often differences between what people told police and what they said later during the Reilly hearings. Busboy Stanley Tomaszewski was initially evasive about his actions in the Melody Lounge on the night of the fire. Four times, during his first interview with police on November 29, the day after the fire, police captain John F. McCarthy point-blank asked the boy, "Did you light a match?" Four times, Tomaszewski replied, "No." Only when McCarthy asked the busboy if bartender John Bradley had told him to turn on the light in the palm tree did the sixteen-year-old open up. "He told me to put it on and I said to the party who was at the table, 'You are not allowed to put out any lights. It is too dark.' The party said jokingly, 'Oh, leave it off.' I couldn't see the bulb and I struck a match and put it on and then I stepped away. Then all of a sudden the palm tree seemed to take fire." Pressed as to whether the match caused the fire, Stanley said defensively, "Well, it didn't start right away." McCarthy pushed him: "So that this fire started at the Cocoanut Grove, Stanley, as the result of your lighting a match?"

"I believe so," the boy replied.

A day later, when questioned by Commissioner Reilly, Tomaszewski acknowledged that he had held onto the match until he got to the floor, when he stepped on it. When Reilly asked, "Do you think that match caught fire to the tree?" the boy replied, "It probably did." One thing to keep in mind is that on November 30, Stanley may not have known what happened to his friend Joseph Tranfaglia or just learned he had died. He may also have been scared by the police: the first question was "Are you Polish?"

Bartender John Bradley was likewise inconsistent about whether he saw the man undo the light bulb in the palm tree or Stanley told him about it. He was even evasive about ordering Stanley to put it in. Bradley said he recalled saying, "It had to be done." It was clear, however, that both he and Stanley tried desperately to put out the fire once it started.

A more concise statement to police came from eighteen-year-old Joyce R. Spector, who said she was sitting near a party of two men and two women, all drunk, when one of them unscrewed the bulb, saying it was too light there. Why did they do that? "Drunks never had any motive," she replied. The Melody Lounge was already dimly lit ("the place is so dark, you wouldn't know your own sister"), and she watched Stanley attempt to put the bulb back in and lit a match to see where it should go. "I kept watching him very closely because we were amused at the whole situation and we watched him and the bulb was in already and everyone breathed a sigh of relief and then we saw it, Justin [her fiancé] and I saw the palm tree immediately catch fire." Spector barely escaped; she went upstairs and was pulled along by the crowd the length of the dining room to the Shawmut Street exit. She was knocked down and crawled, flame licking her, as people stepped over her. She was finally pulled out by her hair.

The Reilly hearing called in survivors and witnesses as well as Boston officials. Boston building inspector Theodore Eldracher, decorator Reuben Bodenhorn and Lieutenant Frank Linney testified. As reporters scribbled notes, Jean Termine of the North End said she saw a club employee "stand in front of the door—hold out his arms—and tell people that all bills must be paid before leaving." Maurice Levy related watching the busboy light the match in the Melody Lounge and how he lost his wife in the stampede to the revolving door. Others described the panic amid the maelstrom of heat and smoke. It was a litany of the lucky, the stories of those who lived to talk.

Joseph F. Kelley, a building contractor, spoke precisely. The fire "was bluish with a yellow cast as if something were burning in suspension. It wasn't burning at any particular point. The air was full of flame yet the walls and ceiling were not then on fire," he testified. As the ball of fire passed from the foyer into the main dining room, it "leveled out on the ceiling. The flames passed over my head in the passageway and went into the new lounge." Asked to describe the smoke's odor, Kelley said, "It was like nothing I have ever known. I have had a rasping feeling in my throat and chest and food hasn't tasted the same." His companion Benjamin Wheaton described seeing smoke that "rolled up as a wave would roll in from the ocean."

James Welansky gave vague, even sullen responses to Reilly's questions and to police. Asked who took care of fireproofing decorations, he replied, "The decorators. I don't know too much about those things. I'm just giving you my supposition." He also said he didn't know exactly how he got out: "I seemed to be pushed along and carried out." He insisted the club was "crowded but not overcrowded."

The Reilly witnesses gave Boston a glimpse into the heart of the inferno. The normally ebullient Mickey Alpert, his hands bandaged and his face haggard, gave a dazed and confusing story. The former master of ceremonies said that after he realized there was a fire, not a fight, he tried to get out a service door behind the stage. It was locked, but then people pushed it open. He talked about opening another door only to find flames behind it. He also recalled breaking bars on a downstairs window and pushing people through. Then he was trying to make it up the stairs but faltered: "I gave up. I said, 'This is it.' The next thing I know [Civil Defense Director] John Walsh is smacking me in the kisser."

Perhaps the most sensational testimony in the Reilly hearings came from Charlestown sign maker Henry Weene, who testified that he warned Barney Welansky that a master electrician should be engaged to do the wiring in the new Broadway lounge. "Welansky said it was not necessary because Mayor Tobin and I fit," Weene told investigators, adding that he replied, "That doesn't cover me much." Many seized on the oddly phrased comment as evidence of the complicity of higher-ups in the Cocoanut Grove management. Mayor Maurice Tobin himself first ignored Weene's testimony, but as the outrage increased, he issued a statement saying Barney Welansky had no right to make such a statement "any more than any other man in business has a right to make any other similar statement with regard to me."

Other revelations about the club's furnishings and electrical wiring followed. Boston Police archives contain a chilling December 2, 1942 transcript of the questioning of Raymond Baer, an unlicensed electrician who installed electrical fixtures in the Broadway lounge without proper

Investigators sift through debris from the club hoping to find evidence on the cause of the fire. *Courtesy of Boston Public Library.*

permits. Under questioning, Baer admitted that after he had been working at the club for six weeks, Barney and contractor Samuel Rudnick talked "about no permit being on the job and Mr. Rudnick said it would all be taken care of." Pressed as to why he would proceed when he knew the work was illegal, Baer just repeated, "Things were said that everything was taken care of."

But things were not "taken care of." The club's wiring did not, to put it in legal terms, "conform to good practices." Bernard Welan, superintendent of the fire department wiring division, said during the Reilly hearings he had sent notices on November 7 and November 17 warning the new lighting system was illegal, as the proper permits had not been obtained.

The club's decorations were also suspected of causing or fueling the inferno. On December 2, state chemists announced they tested fifteen of the materials in the club, including fabric from the Melody Lounge, the fake palm tree leaves and wrapping, red imitation leather on the walls and chairs in the dining room. They found much of the material highly flammable; the palm tree wrapping material, for example, "burst into violent flames instantly, in much the same manner as a dry Christmas tree." Fabric used in the club also ignited almost instantly and "was entirely consumed." Bodenhorn's fashionable leatherette covering burned quickly with "very irritating, acrid fumes." The palm tree leaves, surprisingly, showed the most resistance to flames, but the chemist concluded that the majority of the material was not currently flame resistant, although they could not determine if the materials had been treated in the past.

Even as city leaders vowed to fully investigate the tragedy, a sense of fatalism set in. Letters to newspapers seethed with rage and predicted that the tragedy would be swept under the rug, that the guilty would wiggle free. "Do 500 people have to be killed before they get out of their warm offices and do some investigating? In a small town everyone is afraid of the big shots," Phil Connell wrote to the *Boston Globe* a few days after the fire. "The Cocoanut Grove mass murder is the result of Boston's notoriously rotten politics," declared Eugene Willard in a December 14 letter to the *Globe*.

Indeed, city officials were running for cover. "Three Boards Deny Responsibility" was the *Daily Record* headline three days after the fire, a day

The fire started in this corner of the Melody Lounge in a palm tree, according to witnesses. This photo was taken during the investigation and saved by retired Boston firefighter and photographer Bill Noonan. *Courtesy of Bill Noonan.*

after the city's licensing board, the building department and the Boston Police Department all said they had "no power to alter the condition of the building." The only person who appeared to be forthright about his involvement was young Stanley Tomaszewski, who told investigations he thought his match might have ignited the palm tree and set the club on fire.

Even as he was conducting his investigation, Reilly found himself answering questions from state prosecutors who had convened a grand jury. Massachusetts attorney general Robert Bushnell kicked off a criminal investigation at the direction of Governor Leverett Saltonstall with state fire marshal Stephen C. Garrity directing the effort; state police detective lieutenant Philip W. Deady was assigned as principal investigator.

As the criminal investigation and the Reilly hearings continued, the rotten heart of Boston's number one glitter spot was gradually exposed. Investigators poking in the ruins found one of Barney Welansky's secrets: a huge cache of more than four thousand cases of assorted liquor that had been hidden in the cellar under a trap door and lacked government tax seals. Welansky was apparently trying to dodge paying taxes on the booze. On December 11, investigators found a bricked-up door in the wall at the end

Barney Welansky (*right*), owner of the Cocoanut Grove. *Courtesy of Bill Noonan and the Boston Public Library.*

of the Caricature Bar, an exit that would have provided an outlet to those caught on that side of the club. Welansky insisted it had been bricked up by the owner of a parking space who complained about club staff hanging around outside.

Local newspapers competed to find the latest developments. One reporter dug deep into the past to explain the present. Austen Lake, a scribe for the *Record American* with a jaunty, evocative style, had a way of injecting himself into his stories. He focused his hard-edge energy on the Cocoanut Grove. He toured the wreckage of the building and helped produce a diagram of the complex. He claimed to establish "beyond question" that the interior hanging fabrics—which were supposed to be treated with flame retardant—were "not even remotely fireproof." The tests were not exactly scientific—Lake helped himself to eight materials on the site, held a match to each, and all "burned with an immediate, all-consuming intensity." More tellingly, Lake seized on the club's history as evidence that the fire was the inevitable consequence of corruption and greed. In style long on flourish and somewhat stingy with facts, he wrote a multipart series on "The Rise and Fall of the Cocoanut Grove," which recounted the tale of Mick Alpert, Jack Berman, King Solomon and the Welanskys in a feverish rant, as if information was personally transmitted by divine dictation.

For all his hyperbolic style, Lake hit a nerve. On December 14, the *Record* reported Lake received threats and a phone call to "go easy" on the Cocoanut Grove. His editors (or Lake himself) wrote a defiant note, printed on December 16, saying that "you are hereby notified that on the contrary, Austen Lake will pull the lid off the situation in back of Cocoanut Grove." The threatening phone call had been traced, and "we are ready for you." Such posturing might be dismissed as a paper-selling ploy, but the investigation had rattled someone. The lead state police investigator, Philip Deady, received death threats; his son had to go to school under armed guard for a time. Even Jacques Renard, long gone from the club, was contacted and told to keep quiet, Edith Nussinow told this author. Renard even felt he could never go back to Boston. Frank Shapiro, who later acted as a lawyer for the victims, also said he received menacing phone calls, and decades later he refused to speculate on who had made them.

Perhaps someone was worried about a box of unpaid food and liquor checks, signed off by Grove management, for the "right people," confiscated by authorities on December 4. The bundle of meal and liquor checks also included notations, such as "important," "a good friend" and "see me" and "will settle later." Asked whose names were on the chits, a detective replied,

James Welansky, brother of owner Barney, who was in the club the night of the fire. *Courtesy of the Boston Public Library, Leslie Jones Collection.*

"Names of some witnesses, you'll not ask us how to spell when you hear them." The box subsequently disappeared, Deady's son, Jack, recalled.

On December 31, 1942, indictments were handed down. Ten people were eventually prosecuted in several separate legal actions. Charged with involuntary manslaughter in the most serious case were the brothers Welansky and wine steward Jacob Goldfine, who was considered to be, with James Welansky, in charge of the club that night. Prosecuted in separate actions on charges ranging from conspiracy to violate building codes to willful neglect of duty were club designer Reuben Bodenhorn, Boston fire lieutenant Frank J. Linney (who had found conditions at the club "good"), Boston police captain Joseph Buccigross (who was in the club while he was supposed to be making his inspection rounds), Boston building commissioner James Mooney, building inspector Theodore Eldracher and contractors David Gilbert and Samuel Rudnick.

The Welanskys-Goldfine manslaughter trial began on March 15, 1943, with Judge Joseph L. Hurley presiding. Attorney General Robert T. Bushnell brought the charges in the name of nineteen victims, including Eleanor Chiampa, Adele Dreyfus and Anna Stern from the Buck Jones party.

They were carefully chosen for their cause of death and locations in the club. Bushnell argued that the defendants caused the deaths by "willfully, wantonly and recklessly maintaining, managing, operating and supervising" the club. Wisely, the prosecution did not focus on the cause of the fire, which had not been officially determined; rather, they emphasized the unsafe conditions—the inadequate number of exits, the locked doors, the unlicensed electrical work and the flammable furnishings. By the time the trial ended on April 10, 327 witnesses had testified, and 131 exhibits were shown to the jury, including a burned palm tree, the center post of the revolving door and boxes of wires, carried in by State Police Lieutenant Philip Deady.

Barney Welansky was defended by his law partner, Herbert F. Callahan, who tried to portray his client as a hardworking businessman who had no way of preventing the mad stampede in the inferno. Goldfine and James Welansky, defended by two other lawyers, Daniel J. Gallagher and Abraham C. Webber, did not testify in their defense. Barney did, dissolving in tears on the stand, as Bushnell conducted a punishing cross-examination. Bushnell

A view of the main dining room toward the entrance to the Broadway Lounge shows the amount of material left unburned and the one area where the roof collapsed. *Courtesy of Bill Noonan.*

pushed the club owner hard over the question of why the exit door near the Melody Lounge was locked shut the night of the fire; indeed, a firefighter testified he had to force the door open.

Bushnell: "Whose responsibility was it to keep that door open for members of the public whom you invited to the Cocoanut Grove so that you should make money—whose responsibility was it?"

Welansky: "I told Balzarini [the head waiter] to keep that door open."

Bushnell: "You knew there was a panic bolt on that door?"

Welansky: "Yes."

Bushnell: "How did it happen that in addition to a panic lock there was a tongue lock on that door?"

Welansky: "I can't explain it. I don't know who did it."

Callahan hammered on a lack of evidence: "There is no evidence that anyone tried to use the Melody Lounge door. There is no evidence that Welansky ever ordered that the door be locked." In his summation, Callahan argued that Welansky could not have anticipated a conflagration that started a mass panic.

The prosecution pressed on the licensing dodges. Wiring inspector Frank H. Kelly testified that he discovered that electrical work was being done without a permit in the new cocktail lounge in early November 1942. He said that two violation notices had been sent out. Under cross-examination, however, he said the general wiring conditions were "very good." Sign maker Weene testified on March 25 about Barney Welansky's purported statement that he and Mayor Tobin fit. Weene retorted, "That doesn't help me much," but the club owner waved his hand and said, "They owe me plenty" and walked away. Callahan insisted Welansky never said anything like that and sought to undercut Weene's credibility.

The key element in Callahan's defense strategy was that patrons caused their own death by panicking instead of exiting calmly: "You heard a witness say: 'It was every man for himself.' People were acting like wild animals. People were knocked down and trampled on. Many who did use their heads did get out. It was an occasion of terror, and once terror prevails, there is no telling what can happen." He continued, "Only yesterday you heard of five men sitting at a table with five women. The men tipped the table over on the women in their haste to escape. Once panic strikes, safety devices mean nothing at all. They are virtually useless."

The closing arguments for the prosecution were given by assistant district attorney Frederick T. Doyle, who, according to reporters, "delivered his argument in a thunderous voice that gave spectators the impression he certainly was being heard down in Scollay Square." Barney Welansky "rigged the whole situation," with Goldfine as his right-hand man and brother James in control while Barney was in the hospital, Doyle told the jury. The club was, he said, "hermetically sealed." Patrons should have easily escaped via the panic lock in the Melody Lounge exit; instead "it was a phony. It was bolted."

"Why was it kept locked? To keep some kid from slipping out without paying his check? We know it was locked. We know bodies were piled there....To say this is an accident is ludicrous. Those responsible for that trap are sitting in the dock....Someone said those who used their heads got out. James Welansky got out. Jacob Goldfine got out. But did the poor souls named here get out? It's a libel on the dead."

Doyle was relentless. "All day you have been filled up with smooth talk about panic. What did they expect the people to do? Stand up and be burned to death? They ran to one door. It was locked. They ran to another. It was locked."

Never mind about the busboy's match—greed caused the fire: "They were not content with an income of $1,000 a night. They blocked up an exit with a coat rack at a dime a head. There wasn't a penny to be lost. It was absolute greed and avarice. They were not content with the average flow of trade. Instead of advertising their 'breathtaking' cocktail lounge, they should have advertised: 'Come to the Grove and abandon hope.'"

In his nearly two-hour charge to the jury, Judge Hurley warned that this case "is not an attempt to find someone on whom to pin the blame. It is not an attempt to find a scapegoat for public vengeance to be inflicted upon." Nor was it, he insisted, an investigation into the cause of the fire. The jury was out for four hours and fifty minutes. They returned with the verdict: Jacob Goldfine: Not guilty. James Welansky: Not guilty. Barney Welansky: Guilty.

The verdict set a legal precedent for involuntary manslaughter caused through wanton or reckless conduct. While usually reckless conduct involved an affirmative act, like driving a car, the Welansky case determined reckless conduct, as distinguished from mere negligence, involved intentional failure to ignore potentially harmful conditions, such as fire from any cause. On April 14, an emotionless Barney Welansky was sentenced to twelve to fifteen years, the "first 24 hours in solitary confinement and the residue at hard labor." Welansky was led away in manacles, the one person to be held responsible for so many problems. "It's too bad Barney has to take the rap," said Goldfine, and other employees agreed. Welansky appealed, but his conviction was upheld.

The remains of the revolving door. *Courtesy of Bill Noonan.*

The Welansky conviction set a precedent that has reverberated over the years. Attorney John C. Esposito, who studied the case during law school, has always been fascinated by it. In 2006, Esposito, who served as chief counsel to the New York State Consumer Protection Board for five years, published *Fire in the Grove: The Cocoanut Grove Tragedy and Its Aftermath*, a gripping account of the fire and its legal implications. He writes: "The court's landmark decision took the law of involuntary manslaughter beyond the realm of driving a car or firing a gun recklessly. No longer was involuntary manslaughter limited to acts that led directly to the injury or death in question: it now clearly extended to disregard for the safety of others to whom one has a duty of care."

This was not an entirely new concept, Esposito acknowledges. The issue of ownership culpability was raised in trials over the deadly 1911 Triangle Shirtwaist Factory fire in New York and the 1903 Iroquois Theatre fire, which left more than six hundred people dead. However, in both cases there were acquittals. "The case of Commonwealth v. Welansky moved the law beyond these early cases. It marked the first time an appellate court has so clearly and comprehensively defined the law of involuntary manslaughter especially in the context of multiple deaths in places of public assembly," Esposito noted. *Commonwealth v. Welansky* has been cited in cases such as the 2003 deadly fire at the Station Nightclub in Rhode Island and other cases in which corporations can be held liable for deadly "accidents."

In other court actions, Inspector Linney was acquitted of willful neglect of duty in November 1943. In July 1944, charges were dropped against Buccigross, and he was reinstated to duty; he eventually won back pay for the nineteen months he was suspended. Charges of conspiracy to violate building laws were dropped against building inspector James H. Mooney; Bodenhorn, Eldracher and Gilbert were acquitted of charges. Rudnick was convicted of conspiracy to violate building laws, sentenced to two years and paroled in October 1945 after serving six months in state prison.

If greed caused the Grove fire, greed continued to poison the lives of its victims. Money, jewelry and personal items were looted from the bodies of victims, denying relatives mementos such as wedding rings and jewelry. More importantly, the club was found to be woefully underinsured. The six insurance companies involved paid out only $22,420 for damage to the club's contents; Welansky had not bothered to get liability insurance. The club building itself was deemed worthless. About five hundred injured and families of the dead filed about $8 million in damages against the club; some lawyers labeled the suits "outrageous."

To sort out claims, prominent lawyer Lee M. Friedman was named receiver of the club; Friedman turned to a young associate, Frank H. Shapiro, the passerby who had pulled victims from the fire. Shapiro was told to drop all his cases, and for more than two years, he worked on the nightclub case. It was, he recalled sixty-two years later in an interview with this author, "a nightmare." The club's ownership—needed to establish liability—was a tangled web of documents, the club property itself was practically worthless and the insurance payoffs were negligible. Moreover, Shapiro received threatening phone calls, telling to keep his mouth shut about documents found at the club. "You're a nice young lawyer. You can live a nice long life," the voice on the phone sneered. For a year, he and his wife lived under police guard.

The hidden cache of liquor was auctioned, with the intent that the $171,000 in proceeds go to victims. But the federal government, which had charged Barney Welansky for tax evasion, demanded taxes be paid on the liquor as well as on the sale of the Grove land, as part of the Grove's assets. The government wanted $200,000, which would have left nothing for victims. After years of negotiation, the government reduced its claims by half, leaving $100,000 available for victims. In the end, survivors received only about $100 apiece for their pain and suffering, a "pittance" as Shapiro put it. The hospitals bore much of the treatment costs, and the Red Cross pitched in with grants and other services. One of the Red Cross's roles was to reassure victims that they would get medical care; many were frantic about how they would pay for their treatment.

Still, bitterness among the survivors was palpable. Joseph Dreyfus, the medical student who lost his wife in the fire, spent six weeks nearly unconscious in Boston City Hospital, and for a while he thought he had been blinded. Even after he recovered enough to resume his internship, every time he scrubbed for an operation, his gloves would be filled with blood. While Dreyfus's hospitalization was covered, his father spent $50,000 on private nurses to take care of him in the three to four months he was recovering at home. "When they finally settled the estate of the Cocoanut Grove, I got a hundred dollars," he told Charles C. Kenney Jr. Joseph Dreyfus continued his medical training and was considered a burn expert. "What I did, a month after I got on my feet, was to go to a nightclub."

The boarded, burned-out shell of the club, still attracting the curious, remained until 1945, when it was torn down. As workmen began to dismantle the building, they found eerie mementos of the inferno—a wallet, an inscribed watch and a ticket stub to the Boston College–Holy Cross game. Even as the Grove disappeared, it yielded a last mystery.

Acting on a tip, in June 1945, police investigated the ruins and discovered that someone had entered the building and emptied a safe that had been hidden in a wall under the stairs to the Melody Lounge. Barney Welansky claimed to know nothing about it, saying the safe must have been a leftover from the King Solomon days. After waiting two and half years, the burglars tore out a large section of a wall leading to the safe, drilled it open and vanished, leaving it empty. Its contents—if any—remain a mystery.

Barney Welansky didn't serve out his jail term. In late November 1946, dying from lung and trachea cancer, the former club owner was pardoned by Maurice Tobin, who had been elected governor of Massachusetts in 1944 but lost his reelection bid. Leaving prison, Welansky defended his release, saying, "If you were wrongfully convicted—framed—you'd feel you had a perfect right to be free." Tears came to his eyes, and he added, "I only wish I had been at the fire and died with those others." He died two months later, in January 1947.

9

WHAT CAUSED THE FIRE?

*After exhaustive study and careful consideration of all the evidence, and after
many personal inspections of the premises, I am unable to find precisely and
exactly the immediate cause of this fire.*
—*Report by State Fire Marshal Stephen C. Garrity, November 13, 1942*

The question has been pondered for years. What caused the Cocoanut
Grove Fire? Was it the match lit by the busboy? Or was something
else at work? Initial witness accounts, including the busboy's own
reckoning, would indicate that the fire was inadvertently started by busboy
Stanley Tomaszewski, something that would dog him for the rest of his life.
Yet as soon as a few days after the fire, many began to question if one single
match could have caused such havoc.

Tomaszewski's manner and honesty about lighting the match won him
support among police, investigators and even Fire Commissioner Reilly.
Authorities placed him in protective custody. A wise move, as family and
friends of the victims were crying for vengeance, their grief spilling into
anger. On Monday, "Police Say Busboy's Match Caused Fire" blazed across
the front page of the *Boston Globe*. Stanley's ailing mother cried over and over
again to reporters, "Stanley is a good boy," while crowds gathered outside
her home to denounce her son.

Within a week, doubts were raised about Stanley's match, no matter
how straightforward his story seemed. A little over a week after the fire, on
December 7, "Busboy Did Not Start Fire: Hidden Blaze Raged in Walls"
blared the headline of the *Boston American*.

This photo of the wreckage of the main dining room shows some of the mysteries of this fire. Note the number of combustible decorations—including palm trees with their fake fronds intact. *Army Signal Corps/Courtesy of Boston Public Library.*

Many witness statements to both police and the Reilly Commission in the month after the fire were confusing and contradictory. Some witnesses said they did not see the match ignite the tree, rather they saw sparks after Stanley screwed in the light bulb. Stanley thought he carefully extinguished the match. Others described seeing a "flash." Other clubgoers told of being so hot in the Melody Lounge that the walls themselves seemed to radiate heat. A bit of the palm tree where the fire supposedly started was still intact—surely that would have been consumed first? As photos of the ruined club show, a tremendous amount of what would be considered flammable material was left after the fire. Chairs, bottles, bongo drums, even sheet music remained unburned in the rubble.

"Much of the cloth, rattan and bamboo contained in the Melody Lounge, and on the sides and lower walls of the stairway leading from there, was, in fact, not burned at all and the same is true of carpet on the stairway, contrary to all usual fire experience," Reilly wrote in his sixty-four-page report on the fire issued on November 19, 1943.

Clubgoers clearly saw a fireball, a flash of fire roar through the club, yet the club itself did not reach what fire protection professionals call "flashover," in which the heat of a fire rises so high that everything inside a room ignites and is consumed. The Station Nightclub Fire of February 20, 2003, in West Warwick, Rhode Island, which killed about one hundred people inside the club, is a clear example of flashover.

Some have speculated that faulty wiring was the cause. Testimony indicated that Welansky had cut corners by hiring unlicensed electricians. Lieutenant Philip Deady, the lead investigator for the state fire marshal's office, always harbored suspicions about wiring, telling his son that "ignition was caused by a probable short circuit in the faulty, jerry-rigged wiring behind the false wall of the Melody Lounge, which cause a shower of sparks to escape through the air space between the false wall and true ceiling of the room onto the cotton 'satin' ceiling covering….This fabric burned with incredible rapidity, almost like an explosive fuse, involving the entire room in only a few minutes." Likewise, contractor Joseph Kelley, who escaped from the club, initially told

A view of the main dining room toward the entrance to the Broadway lounge shows the one area where the roof collapsed. *Photo courtesy of Bill Noonan.*

police that the fire "could have only been caused by a short circuit under the bar in the Melody Lounge....In my opinion, a short circuit was spread down through and caused the wiring to set up spontaneous combustion. I never saw anything get going so sudden. There was so much smoke. But whatever happened, happened awfully fast."

That frightful speed made many believe some kind of accelerant was at work. Said Reilly: "The substance of the fire was a highly heated, partially burned but still burning, compressed volume of gas. By its nature this gas pressed for every available opening, and I have found that this was the cause of its rapid course throughout the premises." The search for the mysterious accelerant—perhaps the same as the "mystery gas" that caused lung injuries—has inspired a range of theories, from the realistic to the outlandish. Among the theories: Gasoline fumes, from the club's day as a garage, had caught fire. Film stock, known to be flammable, might have been stored on the premises. Fumes from the large amount of alcohol being consumed were ignited. Reporter Austen Lake suggested that Nazi saboteurs, known to be operating on the East Coast, had set the fire; he didn't publish this theory, however, until 1964, indicating that even this tabloid writer couldn't bring himself to believe it. A theory that Welansky's underworld enemies set the fire has also been floated.

In his final report, Reilly absolved Tomaszewski of blame for the fire, writing: "After a careful study of all the evidence, and an analysis of all the facts presented before me, I am unable to find the conduct of this boy was the cause of the fire." He concluded, "This fire will be entered in the records of this department as being of unknown origin." State fire marshal Stephen Garrity also reached a similar roadblock. In a November 8, 1943 letter to Massachusetts governor Leverett Saltonstall, Garrity said that after examining Tomaszewski's testimony, "it is clear to me that he did not ignite the palm tree in the Melody Lounge and thereby cause the fire." In a separate report, Garrity concluded, "I am unable to find precisely and exactly the immediate case of this fire."

Robert Moulton, technical secretary of the National Fire Protection Association—an international nonprofit fire protection and prevention organization—wrote a detailed analysis of the fire published about a year after the tragedy. The fire "could have perhaps been started by defective amateur wiring to the fixture in the [palm] tree instead of by the [busboy's] match," he wrote. As for the cause of the fire's "incredible rapidity" and a supposed mysterious lethal gas, Moulton considered and rejected various theories, including gasoline fumes or leftover scraps of flammable motion picture film. "All the facts can perhaps be accounted for without seeking any mysterious or unusual explanation," Moulton wrote. "The combustible decorations, cloth finish on the ceiling and other readily combustible material could have caused a quick, hot and fast-spreading fire. Lung injuries could be explained by the inhalation of ordinary smoke and superheated air."

Many fire experts, including several who fought the blaze, believe the most logical explanation is still that the busboy's match was the spark that quickly ignited the fabric covering the ceiling of the Melody Lounge. Some speculate that the stairway to the Melody Lounge acted as a kind of chimney to pull heat and flame upward. Witness Maurice Levy, who lost his wife in the fire, was furious that anyone would doubt that the fire was caused by Stanley's match. He angrily told a reporter he saw how the fire started and that his "testimony was completely ignored."

Nearly thirty years after the fire, in 1970, the Boston Fire Department again attempted to pinpoint a cause. Boston district fire chief John P. Vahey, a well-respected veteran firefighter, as well as a fire historian, carefully reexamined the evidence. In his report, "Design for Disaster," published by the Boston Sparks Association, he, once more, found Tomaszewski's conduct blameless. He concluded the department was "unable to determine the original cause or causes of the fire." Without an official explanation, the busboy with the match remains the most logical explanation.

Following a commemoration of the fiftieth anniversary of the fire, another theory emerged. Two fire historians—Charles C. Kenney, a former Boston firefighter and son of Boston firefighter Charles Kenney Sr., who rescued Dotty Myles at the fire, and Jack Deady, son of investigator Philip Deady—came to believe a refrigerant gas was the initial accelerant that ignited and raced through the club.

Moulton of the NFPA had ruled out refrigerator gas as an accelerant, saying none of the commonly used refrigerant gasses were flammable or toxic. In 1992, Kenney was contacted by a retired Cambridge refrigerator repairman who had, as a young man working with his father, seen the club's refrigerator unit after it was removed from the club to his father's refrigerator service business in Cambridge, Massachusetts. Walter Hixenbaugh, now living in Florida, told Kenney he was certain that the unit was not using the common gas freon as a coolant but instead the gas methyl chloride; freon was in short supply due to the war. He also saw small leaks in the unit's condenser tubing. At the time, Hixenbaugh was shipped overseas to fight in World War II, so he was not in Boston for the nightclub investigation or trial. Hixenbaugh wondered if the methyl chloride could explain the fire's rapid spread.

Interestingly, this was not the first mention of methyl chloride in connection with the Cocoanut Grove.

In the Boston Fire Department's archives, Kenney found a December 4, 1942 letter to reporter Austen Lake from W. Irving Russell, a radio and refrigerator serviceman, who had read Joseph Kelley's testimony during Reilly's hearings. He had written to Lake "in regard to the so called 'Mystery Gas'" to suggest that methyl chloride may have been substituted for freon and that "a leak of this gas would produce conditions exactly as obtained in the Cocoanut Grove on the night of the fire." Lake, despite his vow to "blow the lid" off the Grove case, had not followed up on the tip.

Methyl chloride is, according to a "Hazardous Materials" notebook series published in *Fire Engineering* in June 1989, "a flammable, toxic, corrosive, narcotic, clear, colorless gas with a sweet aroma similar to ether." It is usually stored and shipped as a liquid under pressure, and "any liquid that is released will involve tremendous quantities of flammable, toxic, and corrosive gas." After talking with Hixenbaugh, Kenney came to believe a refrigerator unit behind a wall in the Melody Lounge was supplied with methyl chloride, not freon because of the wartime demand for freon. When the refrigerator unit leaked, the gas pooled and was ignited by an electrical spark, thus providing the accelerant that blew through the building and created the bluish flame that Kelley described. This accelerant ignited the flammable fabric ceiling and the leatherette coverings, which burned rapidly. Kenney argues that the floor plans of the club, made in December 1942, showed a "fan compressor room" behind the false wall in the Melody Lounge at the fire's original point. Yet the floor plans submitted in Reilly's report did not indicate this room. The compressor-condenser from the refrigerator unit was removed from the lounge during the investigation and subsequently disappeared. Jack Deady, moreover, believes photos of the northwest corner of the lounge show that fire started behind the wall and burned into the room.

The theory has intrigued fire professionals. In 1996, Doug Beller, a National Fire Protection Association fire modeling specialist, created a computer model of the Cocoanut Grove case that examined the methyl chloride theory. He found the new theory explained some of the lingering mysteries of the fire but not all. Methyl chloride may act as a depressive—victims talked about becoming sluggish and passing out. The gas emits a sweet odor—something many victims recalled. Short-term exposure causes a bluish skin color; many victims were found with bluish skin tone thought to be oxygen deprivation.

Methyl chloride's thermal decomposition products include phosgene—the gas suspected of causing pulmonary edema in patients. Also, alcohol may enhance the chemical's toxic effects.

However, Beller noted that methyl chloride is heavier than air. This would not explain why flames were first seen in the palm tree fronds or the rolling waves of fire that spread along the ceiling of the lounge and into the main dining room. According to a 1993 Boston Fire Department statement to the NFPA, the density of methyl chloride is 1.7 times greater than air and "is inconsistent with this gas causing the observed spread of time along the ceiling in the Melody Lounge." Ultimately, Beller could not come to a conclusion that this was the accelerant.

The speculation on the cause of the fire, however, misses the point. Fires start all the time in all kinds of places for reasons known and unknown. But they don't kill nearly five hundred people, most of whom were frantically trying to get out of the club. The cause of the disaster was, in the final analysis, not the match but the conditions of the club.

In March 2022, I spoke at length with Casey Grant, a fire engineering professional and the retired executive director of the Fire Protection Research Foundation, NFPA's research affiliate. He has studied the Cocoanut Grove fire at length and spoken and written extensively about its dynamics. I have talked to Casey many times over the years, and I sought his help again for the update of this book. He addressed the lingering questions: "No matter how this fire started, whether it's electrical or a match, why did it spread the way it did? And why couldn't people get out? We know the answer to the latter part of that. They couldn't get out because every exit out of that place had something functionally wrong with it, every single one."

The nightclub was not adhering to well-established fire and life safety codes that existed at that time. The death and injury totals would have been reduced had the panic bar in the door at the top of the stairs from the Melody Lounge worked or had the revolving doors of the main entrance not jammed. The locked doors in the dining room on the Shawmut side and behind the stage and the inward-opening door of the new Broadway lounge sealed the fate of so many patrons.

Grant remains baffled by how rapidly the fire spread. In just over five minutes, a ball of fire spread from the downstairs Melody Lounge through the Caricature Bar and main dining room, through a hallway and into the Broadway lounge—about 225 feet away, as described in Commissioner Reilly's Report from the Boston Fire Department. This is the timetable established by Grant based on multiple sources, including eyewitness testimony and Boston Fire Department records: A small fire was seen in the palm tree in the downstairs Melody Lounge at 10:15 p.m. Within a minute, it was a large fire that ignited the cloth ceiling of the lounge. By about 10:19 p.m., the fire had traversed the foyer and entered the Caricature Bar. By 10:20, it was roaring through the main dining room and entering the Broadway lounge. By 10:21, fire was shooting out of the Broadway lounge. By 10:23, the fire was advancing throughout the club, and from 10:25 to 10:30 it burned throughout the structure even as heavy lines of water were employed by firefighters. By 10:45, a full rescue operation was underway, dealing with the human wreckage as a mass casualty event.

That speed defies fire engineering science. Even using today's forensic tools and computing modeling, the Cocoanut Grove fire did not seem to follow expected fire growth curves, Grant said. In 2014, 2015 and 2017, Grant joined with Professor Nick Dempsey to challenge graduate-level engineering students at Worcester Polytechnic Institute to use computer models of the fire and explain some of its unusual—even bizarre—behavior. A number of factors have emerged.

Grant showed me a presentation slide with a photo of the foyer of the club, taken looking toward the staircase leading to the Melody Lounge. The ceiling here is rounded, not flat, almost like the half barrel of a gun. When a ball of fire barreled up from the Melody Lounge, it whipped through the foyer like "it was shot out of a gun" and into the Caricature Bar, the main dining room and then the new lounge. The configuration of the foyer ceiling is seen to be one reason for this.

What might have saved people in the Broadway lounge was a door between the main dining room and the lounge. Per fire code, it was supposed to be installed and closed. But it was never installed. Had it been in place, it would have surely slowed the spread of fire into Broadway lounge, where hundreds died, Grant said. The subsequent court case that eventually found Grove owner Barney Welansky guilty of criminal negligence focused primarily on this missing door.

Grant showed me a photo of the main dining room next to the Caricature Bar. This was the only spot where the fire burned through the roof to the outside. Just below that spot is the entrance to the Broadway lounge. An exhaust fan in the wall might have also been pulling the fire forward. The fire and heat were intense at this one spot. What intrigued the students—like the initial investigators—was the amount of combustibles remaining in the main dining room and elsewhere, including whole palm trees. What burned was of course of interest, but so too was what didn't burn. Additionally, a

The foyer of the club
looking toward
Church Street

Checkroom

To downstairs
Melody Lounge

To revolving door

This photo, taken during the investigation and saved by Boston Fire Department photographer Bill Noonan, shows the foyer of the Cocoanut Grove and its curved ceiling. The fire moved up from the Melody Lounge into this foyer and then hence into the dining room, which is behind the viewer. *Courtesy of Bill Noonan.*

photo of the ceiling of the Broadway lounge shows the remains of fallen tiles and the drips of glue that had held them there. Tiles used at the time were not combustible, but the glue was—something learned through subsequent disasters and seen in hindsight as a factor.

Another anomaly of this fire is its death toll. In most disasters—as a generalization—there is a smaller portion of fatalities, a larger number of injuries and then a larger subset of escapees. In this fire, the ratio was reversed. "For everybody in the club, two out of four would die, one would be injured and only one would escape unharmed. Those are very bad odds," Grant said.

Even with all the modeling, the cause of the fire and the reasons for its speed remain elusive. Grant said a combination of factors may have been at work, a "classic example of the complexities and amazing dynamics of fire. It was a perfect storm." It's likely the exact synergy that created the inferno will never be fully known.

The wreckage of the Broadway lounge. *Army Signal Corps/Courtesy of Boston Public Library.*

None of the lingering mysteries helped ease Stanley Tomaszewski's private hell. Tomaszewski went on to school, military duty, a marriage and career, never shaking the stigma of being "the busboy with the match" and a murderer in the eyes of some. A few years before his death, Tomaszewski told a reporter, "I wish people would let a dead horse die. I've suffered enough—spit on, called every name in the book and threatened. Phone calls in the middle of the night. It hasn't been easy." Yet "I don't have a sense of guilt, because it wasn't my fault. If I felt guilty I wouldn't be talking to you, my name would not be on the doorbell and in the telephone book. I never backed away." Tomaszewski died on October 20, 1994, at age sixty-eight, still haunted by the demons that he may—or may not—have unleashed. He bore these lifelong torments, something Grove owner Barney Welansky managed to cheat through death.

In November 2010, after a talk in Hull, Massachusetts, on the fire, a bent-over man with thick glasses and thinning gray hair rose to speak, and I realized that he was talking about Stanley Tomaszewski, apparently a relative. I whipped out my phone and caught some of his words on video:

"Stanley was a hard worker," the man said in a quavering yet resolute voice. "His father was unemployed. He was trying to help his mother out. Saturday morning, he would get the wagon out and go selling fruit and vegetables. At night he would go to the Cocoanut Grove, making himself a few bucks. He ended up being a captain in the army and had a very successful life."

The man paused with a mirthless chuckle. He continued. "I visited him so many times, and he felt so bad that he got blamed and people were spitting on him and calling him all hours of the morning to blast him for being the culprit, and it wasn't so. I'm only eighty-nine, and I'm enjoying my life. It's so nice to speak my piece here. God love you, Stanley."

I have not been able to identify this man.

No matter how the fire began, the major causes of death in the Cocoanut Grove were the locked doors, inadequate exits, crowded conditions and a fire that spread so fast it defies the science of fire growth. Whatever the initial spark, greed and thoughtlessness were the real killers.

10

THE STRUGGLE TO RECOVER

The more I think of it, the more I am convinced of the powerful role played
by fate in all our lives. For example, if Buck Jones, the western motion picture
star, had kept to my original schedule, at the time of the fire we would have been
visiting the Buddies' club on Boston Common, where I had arranged for him to
entertain servicemen from 9:30 p.m. on. Instead, because of a bad cold, he asked
me to cancel his final stop on a hectic day-long schedule.
—Martin Sheridan, Chicago Tribune, *November 25, 1962*

F ate. Luck. God's will. Those are words we often hear after a disaster
when we grasp for meaning. In his diary, Boston College fan and former
football player Ned Dullea attempted to find meaning in horror.

"November ends in deep gloom," he wrote. "The Cocoanut Grove fire
was one of the worst disasters in American history. On only three occasions
have fires and explosions taken a greater toll of life. In retrospect, the
unmerciful beating that Holy Cross gave BC was the most wonderful thing
that could have happened. If B.C. had won, or even tied, they would have
been undisputed national champions. The entire squad, with coaches and
officials, were to have attended a victory dinner at the Cocoanut Grove.
Rocco Canale was scheduled to sing a baritone solo. With them would have
been girlfriends, sisters, mothers, wives of coaches and officials, etc. The
stunning defeat led the team to call off the whole affair. The boys went home
to bed to try and forget the debacle. None of the B.C. party went, except
unfortunate Larry Kenney and his little group. Surely this was Providential."

With typical humor, Marty Sheridan had these cards made up to hand out to the nosy. *Photo by author.*

This story—that a humiliating loss saved the lives of the Boston College team and officials—has been repeated so many times that it has become part of the lore of the fire, an indication that no matter how horrible things are, the hand of God is visible.

Trouble is, this story may be a myth.

Newspaper articles suggest Boston College made and kept plans for a victory party at the Statler Hotel (not the Cocoanut Grove) on November 28, an event that Boston mayor Maurice Tobin attended. The Statler was a major hotel in Boston at the time; the building is now the Boston Park Plaza Hotel. A story by Arthur Siegel in the December 11, 1959 *Boston Traveler* insists that the tale that BC had planned a party at the Grove was a "highly romantic legend." Wrote Siegel, "The true facts have the Boston College players never intending to go to the Cocoanut Grove that night. Nor did they cancel their postgame plans one bit. They went to the annual Holy Cross/Boston College dance at the Hotel Statler." The wife of a player told Siegel, "When Boston College lost, everybody felt terrible. But nobody ran away and hid. We went to the Statler and there was a lot of good-natured ribbing. But the music was playing and we were dancing and in a couple of hours the game was forgotten and everyone had a wonderful time."

If so, then how did the legend emerge? On December 1, 1942, *Boston Globe* sportswriter Jerry Nason declared that the 55–12 drubbing "saved the Eagles from a far more terrible fate." Nason quotes Boston College coach Denny Myers as saying that a group of prominent Boston College alumni, "eager to give the team a 'victory' dinner and good time," had invited BC players, coaches and their wives to the Grove; tables were reserved and Rocco Canale, big BC guard, was to sing. Myers, who was speaking at the Fifth Down Club luncheon, said, "The hand of God was in that game somewhere. It was impossible we could be so bad and Holy Cross could be that good unless it was so. As you left the field you had the feeling that there was some reason for this that wasn't obvious."

Over the years, according to Cocoanut Grove researcher David Blaney, players have insisted that there was no victory party planned for the Grove in 1942. What may have happened, he believes, is that some Boston College football players or alumni had made plans to meet up at the Cocoanut Grove later that night after the party at the Statler. The fire prevented that.

"Possibly fueling the rumor that the Grove was the intended victory spot is the fact that in 1941, the celebration following the Eagles 14–13 win over their archrivals was indeed held at 17 Piedmont Street," Blaney said.

Yet the story that Boston College was saved from a terrible tragedy by a devastating fire became ingrained in the story of the Grove almost immediately. Dullea, whose brother was the athletic director of Boston College and thus was in a position to know about the party, wrote his entry at the end of November, likely after Nason's story, which also uses the word *providential*. Dullea clearly believed that fate spared Boston College.

This is a very human response. Even amid incomprehensible loss, we seek meaning. Death in the Cocoanut Grove was, in fact, capricious and arbitrary. Some members of a party or family died but not others. Some patrons suffered major injuries; other escaped with only minor injuries. Many survivors had to face these questions: Why did I live? Why did they die? How can I go on with my life?

Somehow people found the strength.

Young Dorothy Myles had extensive burns on her face and hands, severe shock and a cardiac condition that complicated her recovery. A Red Cross report predicted she "may never sing again and if she ever plays the piano in the future, it will not be for a long, long time." As she recovered, scars formed over her face and hands, turning her features into a ghastly surface of pockmarks and cracks. Webs of skin extended to her neck, and her hands were stiff and useless. As the weeks went by, she endured skin graft after skin graft, lying in bed and using the rings on the bed curtain like beads of rosary. She drew strength from meeting Charles Kenney, the fireman who had rescued her and had himself suffered severe lung injuries. On her eighteenth birthday on March 2, she even tried to sing. Though her voice was weak, she had not lost it. After six months in Boston City Hospital, she was discharged.

After 18 Years, Singer Recalls Cry of 'Fire!' at Cocoanut Grove

Philosophy Inspiring To Others

By WILLIAM LONGGOOD, World-Telegram Staff Writer

DOROTHY MYLES.

Dottie Myles underwent numerous operations and was finally able to resume her singing career. But she was haunted by the Grove fire all her life. *Clipping of the* World Telegram, *December 27, 1960, courtesy of Martin Sheridan.*

Even if she had to give up performing in public, she could still sing. Wearing a veil and gloves, she made the rounds of Boston radio stations, where she was hired to do live broadcasts, including the popular WBZ show *Styles by Myles*. She began to receive letters from servicemen who had heard her story and praised her determination. Famed newspaper columnist Damon Runyon, in a 1944 column, cited Myles's courage, writing, "The only fighters are not those in Normandy and the jungles of the Pacific. We've got some great warriors on the home front." Then Myles was introduced to Dr. Varaztad H. Kazanjian, an Armenian immigrant and dentist turned plastic surgeon. While setting jaw fractures, Kazanjian developed new ways of treating jaw injuries. During World War I, he was able to use his skill in prosthetic dentistry to reconstruct the faces of soldiers disfigured during combat. In 1941 he became the first professor of plastic surgery at the Harvard Medical School. And now he was willing to help a victim of the Cocoanut Grove. After a long examination, Dr. Kazanjian's words sent a surge of hope through Dorothy: "There's nothing to worry about so far as your face is concerned. You can be a beautiful girl again."

Myles underwent seventeen operations to rebuild her face. By now all of Boston was rooting for the woman called "Dauntless Dotty." Wearing gloves and with minimal scarring at her throat, she was able to return to a singing career, even appearing in early TV shows in Boston. In the late 1940s and early 1950s, using the name Dorothy McManus (her mother's maiden name), Dorothy discovered another career: singing Irish ballads with Irish bands, including a young Joe Derrane and Connie Foley, in Boston's dance halls. She recorded several records for the Copley record label with an accent so real that many assumed she was born and raised in Ireland. By the late 1950s, she had resumed singing in clubs in New York City. Walter Winchell, in his syndicated column, highlighted Myles's appearance as the "show-stopper" at the Velvet Room, adding, "Champions, as the saying goes, always get up for one more round." Was Captain Robert Morgan's famous B-29 bomber *Dauntless Dotty*, the first Superfortress to bomb Tokyo during World War II, named after Dotty Myles? Myles herself thought so, and Morgan, a well-known rake, implied it in a letter he wrote to Dorothy, saying, "I am proud that my plane can carry the same name as yours," according to a United Press story in February 1945. Yet Morgan said in his biography the plane was named after his first wife, Dorothy.

Myles never could quite escape the psychological damage from the fire. She married and had a daughter, but the marriage went south. According to friends and family, she struggled with alcoholism. A small death notice

Goody Goodelle had what might be called a nervous breakdown after the fire and didn't want to perform again. Yet she recovered and went on to a long career as a singer. *Courtesy of Nora Riva Bergman.*

in the *New York Daily News* of January 24, 1967, reports the sudden death of Dorothy Brown (Dotty Myles) on January 21, leaving behind a daughter, sisters and brothers and her parents.

After the fire, singer Goody Goodelle had what family members describe as a nervous breakdown. She didn't want to play the piano or sing again. She really didn't want to do much of anything. A lot of people thought that she had died in that fire because so many people in the Melody Lounge died, so flowers were arriving at the home along with wires, telegrams and cablegrams. Some days later, a dozen red roses were delivered to her house, and the only thing on the card were the words "Somebody's Thinking of You Tonight." Hoping to cheer up her sister, Riva was determined to track down who sent the roses. Turned out it was a doctor in training named Edgar Yurkanis who had seen her at the Melody Lounge. He convinced her to sing and play the piano again. Uncle Ed, as he would become known, became a lifelong friend of the extended family.

With her sister Riva, Goody sang for children in the hospital. She began performing for returning veterans in the city's hospitals. "She never sings anything sad or nostalgic. Her aim in life is to make people laugh or at least turn their lips up into a smile" wrote Joseph Dinneen, a well-known *Boston Globe* newsman, on June 4, 1945. "When performing at the Circus Room at the Bradford Hotel, men implore her to sing 'Bell Bottom Trousers.'… She will tell you quite simply and directly that she herself is living on borrowed time."

Goody married the night manager of a hotel where she was performing, and they moved to Florida in 1948. She continued to perform, recorded an album of songs written by her husband and became a much-loved regular entertainer in the Fort Lauderdale area.

"The fire event seemed to be pretty intensely emblazoned on her mind. I'm sure she lived with PTSD her whole life," her daughter Nora Riva Bergman told me. "And she was a bit of a worrywart sometimes, which I understand now. You could never take mom to a theater and not have her on an aisle seat. She wanted to know where all the exits were whenever she went somewhere."

Yet Goody went on to have a fulfilling life, filled with music and surrounded by her extended family. Whenever the family returned to Massachusetts, they would visit Uncle Ed. "She was just the most wonderful mom," Bergman said. In 1998, Goody and her sister Riva died together in a tragic car accident in Florida when they were both in their eighties. Bergman still has her mother's baby grand piano.

Other performers resumed their careers: Romeo Ferrara continued to play jazz, and chorus girl Pepper Russell opened a dancing school outside of Boston. She didn't marry her resuscitated beau, Al Willet, who had a long musical career, but the pair stayed friends for life. For years, Jackie Maver worked as a waitress in the Boston area.

Marshall Cole, who escaped without injury, never danced again but retained his ebullient spirits. Joining the U.S. Navy, he served on the USS

Two Cocoanut Grove survivors, Marshall Cole (*left*) and John Rizzo, share a moment during a 2013 ceremony to dedicate the newly named Cocoanut Grove Lane. Both men had vivid memories of escaping the fire. *Photo by author.*

Hancock in the Pacific when the aircraft carrier was targeted by Japanese pilots in kamikaze attacks. Posted as one of three watchmen on a tower, he became ill with what later was diagnosed as meningitis and sought medical attention in sick bay. Had he been at his post, he would have been killed in the kamikaze attack, he told his family. When interviewed by this reporter in 2013, he energetically recounted his experiences the night of the fire, including how he was nearly trapped on the roof and lost his prize possession, his new camel-hair coat. "I'm always looking for an exit. That stuck in my mind until this day. I'm always subconsciously looking for an exit—how to get out." He died on June 28, 2020, at age ninety-four. He, along with former waiter John Rizzo, was featured in the documentary on the Cocoanut Grove fire *Six Locked Doors*.

Bassist Jack Lesberg suffered damage to his lungs and esophagus. For weeks after the fire, he coughed up black soot. He was hospitalized for about a month and for years afterward would suffer anxiety attacks in crowded places. He returned to the burned-out club to see if by some miracle his bass had survived; it had not. He sought a fresh start in New York City and embarked on a long and successful career as a jazz musician, playing with some of the greatest names in the music business, ranging from Louis Armstrong and Benny Goodman to Leonard Bernstein. Lesberg continued to perform well into his eighties. As for the fire's lingering effect, he said simply, "I got to think of myself as a lucky guy." He died in 2005 at age eighty-five after an illustrious career. A curious passage appeared in jazz great Charles Mingus's book *Beneath the Underdog* saying that Lesberg broke through a wall in the Cocoanut Grove using his heavy double bass to escape. Rapper Chuck D reads the passage in the Mingus tribute album *Weird Nightmare*. None of this, however, jives with Lesberg's early accounts. It has become one of the myths of the fire.

After the fire, Mickey Alpert returned to New York City, where he married his longtime girlfriend (who had, coincidentally, been badly burned in another fire) in the home of mutual friend Milton Berle. He launched a career in variety television as a casting director and worked for Berle's Texaco Star Theatre, Jackie Gleason and Ed Sullivan. But he could never escape his memories of the fire. He never talked about that terrible night, but his daughter, Jane, told me that as she was growing up, the fire lurked in the shadows of their family life. Mickey Alpert died in 1965 at age sixty-one. His brother, George Alpert, went on to become president of the New York–New Haven Railroad and a distinguished corporate attorney. (George's son Richard Alpert became the counter-culture guru Baba Ram Dass.)

Five days after the Cocoanut Grove fire, John Quinn was a guard of honor at Dick Vient's funeral; an hour later, he was a pallbearer at Marion Luby's funeral. With burns on his ears still healing, he shipped out a week later. He never saw his beloved Gerry again; she sent him a "Dear John" letter while he was overseas. Quinn came home from the war, a survivor of fire, combat and heartbreak. He went on to civilian life, a marriage and children. Like many survivors, he did not speak of that night in the Grove for years. Then in 1998, his recollection of the fire was printed in *Yankee* magazine. Days later, he got a call from the man who had married Gerry. Gerry had since died, but the man wanted to thank Quinn profusely for his actions that night.

Barney Welansky's nephew Daniel Weiss finished medical school and had a distinguished career as a prominent psychiatrist; he continued to defend his uncle for the rest of his life. Vera Daniels was released from the hospital in June 1943. She eventually received training to become a pathologist; she worked in that capacity at Boston Children's Hospital for twenty-five years. She bore a white scar on her forehead for the rest of her life according to a friend of hers who communicated with Charles C. Kenney.

Buck Jones's agent Scott Dunlap shared a legendary tale. Unconscious from the fumes and smoke, Dunlap awoke to find himself stacked among bodies and someone attempting to get into his pocket. "I'm alive," he managed to cry. "I'll give you $300 to get me to the hospital." Dunlap heard someone say, "Where's the three hundred?" "In my wallet." Dunlap passed out again and awoke in a hospital bed. His wallet contained $500; it *had* contained $800. Dunlap's unusual tale notwithstanding, police reported looting was a major problem in the aftermath of the fire, and many valuable items disappeared, taken from victims who could ill afford to lose anything.

Charles C. Kenney Jr., a former firefighter whose father was at the Cocoanut Grove, became a historian of the fire. Here he is pictured with what he believes are remnants of the cloth that covered the Melody Lounge ceiling. The artifact was donated to the Boston Public Library. *Photo by author.*

Phyllis Capone Cavan was only one and a half years old when her uncle Charlie— Charles Capone—died in the Cocoanut Grove fire. At a 2021 commemoration of the tragedy at the site of the former nightclub, she carried a photo of her uncle. *Photo by author.*

Mario David Capone came home from the war, but the memory of his brother Charlie, who died in the fire, continued to sear the Capone family. Even Charlie's niece and goddaughter, Phyllis Ann, carried with her a memory of loss. "I was a 1½ year old when Uncle Charlie died but he has always been in my heart," she wrote me. For years, the family did not celebrate Thanksgiving, as it was too close to the anniversary of the fire. "The fire was always part of the folklore of the family," said Jim Cavan, the son of Phyllis and grandnephew of Charlie. Cavan, who became a professional paramedic, told me that every time he went to church with his mother, she would pray for Uncle Charlie. During an anniversary commemoration event in 2021 at the site of the fire, she carried a photo of her uncle, regal in a tuxedo with a white carnation in his lapel and smiling with youthful enthusiasm.

Firefighter Charles Kenney didn't want to stay in the hospital, but he had little choice. His lungs had been damaged by the smoke, superheated air and gasses he had inhaled while trying to save as many people as he could. He had a terrible persistent cough that was followed by "an alarming paroxysm" that left him gasping for air. He was also suffering from what today we would call post-traumatic shock. Firefighters didn't get psychological counseling then, just rough-and-rowdy jokes from fellow firefighters who believed in toughing things out. Kenney focused on getting back his physical health—more than anything he wanted to return to his job as a firefighter. His lung injuries made that impossible. At age forty-three, eight days shy of his ten-year anniversary, he retired. As his grandson would write in *Rescue Men*, "The job he loved was taken from him."

As the death toll mounted for the Grove fire—his first fire on his first shift—rookie firefighter John F. Crowley wondered if he had chosen the right profession. "I had to battle within myself as to whether to stay on the job," he wrote in a letter to fire historian Charles C. Kenney Jr. "I stayed. For 31 years."

James Welansky continued to run the Circle Lounge Bar until, ironically enough, it was destroyed by fire in 1961. Welansky died suddenly in April 1962. His obituary claimed that "he helped many persons escape and got out uninjured himself." No mention that he was found not guilty of involuntary manslaughter.

When I was writing my first book in 2003, I had the chance to sit down with Paul Benzaquin, author of the first book on the Cocoanut Grove fire and a veteran reporter and broadcaster. If not for him, so much of what we know about this fire would have been lost. He became interested in the fire as a rookie reporter for the *Boston Globe*. "People would get talking about the big stories and they'd talk about the Grove." He asked the most powerful reporters in the city, "What do you think about a book on the Grove?" and they all said to forget about it. No one would touch it. No one wants to read such a horrible story. But Benzaquin was determined. "I started in 1955 and finished in 1959. I talked to a lot of people. It became sacred to me, and I pursued it. I'm not known for my tenacity of purpose," he added with a laugh, "but I stuck with it."

He tracked down survivors, cajoled them into talking and wrote up their stories with the flare of a novelist. He managed to create a record of experiences that remains unmatched. "I knew some of the people I talked to had fudged their story. They had to. They had to justify their own survival. That was a terrible pain for many people—to come out of the fire alive when their dearest, closest people had died."

I asked him if he thought the fire had been thoroughly investigated at the time. Benzaquin seemed to think not. "You see it was all reflex. It wasn't fully investigated. I don't think they made any determination on how that place could have been in existence in the condition it was and how so many combustible materials could have been used for decorations. And how the fire could have swept through so quickly. Eleven minutes. That's all it took to get that thing roaring."

It turned out that many people wanted to read a "horrible story," and Benzaquin's book became a bestseller. More importantly, he was the first to systematically gather personal stories of the individuals affected by the fire. Paul Benzaquin died on February 13, 2013.

In 2012, this author met Ann Marie Clark Gallagher, the sixteen-year-old who survived the fire, with her younger sister, Carole Robinson, at the offices of the National Fire Protection Association as she prepared to film a video. Ann's face was luminous, her eyes bright and clear and her voice steady. After the fire, she and her sisters were separated. She married and

As a sixteen-year-old, Ann Clark Gallagher survived the fire, but both her parents, her boyfriend and her boyfriend's father died. Here she holds up a photo of her parents during an interview at the National Fire Protection Association headquarters in 2012. *Photo by author.*

had four children, thirteen grandchildren and thirteen great-grandchildren. Her beloved husband, Joe Gallagher, passed away, but she said she felt him watching over her. When I spoke to her, she told me that she had been asked to give out that year's Fred Sharby Jr. trophy, an honor presented every year to a promising football player in Keene, New Hampshire. "I'm so fortunate. I have my sisters and their families. I have wonderful friends. I keep busy, involved in things. I really have a very good life." She still had trouble in crowded places.

Her sister Carole was a baby during the fire, and she, too, dealt with the fallout of losing both parents. She was separated from her sisters and was taken in by various families, none of whom she remembered fondly. One family hid the letters that Ann wrote to her; she only found out about this eight years previous. Carole was finally adopted by a wonderful loving family. Ann Clark Gallagher died in 2017 at age ninety.

But can you outrun fate?

When Coastguardsman Clifford Johnson was still alive after four days, doctors decided they were morally obligated to do everything in their power to help someone with such an incredible will to live. While 45 percent of his skin was lost to third-degree burns and another 15–20 percent had second-degree burns, Johnson's lungs did not have major damage, and his still-handsome face was unscathed. Yet "he could have died at any second without surprising anyone. But he hung on," Benzaquin wrote in an August 31, 1959 *Life* magazine story on Johnson.

Johnson battled off a kidney infection, edema and high fever—he lost more than sixty pounds as protein leached through his system. His team began the painstaking task of skin grafts; they took pinpricks of skin from the few unburned spots on Johnson's body and planted them on the burned area. About six thousand such pinprick grafts were made while Johnson was positioned face-down for six months. Once his upper torso was done, the guardsman, anxious to be in a new position, was turned over. But Johnson had been turned too quickly, within a day, every one of the back skin grafts shifted and sloughed off; all would have to be redone. The blow was devastating to doctors; Johnson, who had valiantly endured the terrible pain and discomforting position, became suicidal. Yet he endured another twenty-five to thirty thousand pinprick skin grafts. Clinicians had no choice but to give him heavy doses of narcotics, knowing that his body would become addicted and he would have to be weaned off the drugs. Every day, the grafts, hardened to tough leather, had to be rubbed with coconut butter to improve elasticity. His unused legs and arms limbered up with physical therapy. To the amazement of his doctors, he improved.

On July 28, 1943, Johnson stood for the first time. His natural ability at flirtation had returned with his strength, and the guardsman was eating up attention from nurses and female visitors. In November 1945, he was discharged from the hospital, his rapturous doctors telling reporters, "We learned more from him about the treatment of burns than has ever been learned from any other single patient." He returned home to Missouri but came back to Boston City Hospital one more time—to fight a recurring bone infection. There he met and wooed a student nurse named Marion Donovan. They were married on September 10, 1946. The couple moved to Missouri, where Johnson worked as a game warden.

Cocoanut Grove survivor Marty Sheridan in 2003 during an interview with the author. Sheridan, a former reporter, wanted to make sure the Boston media never forget about the fire. *Photo by author.*

Clifford Johnson's miraculous story ends on a terrible note. Benzaquin, a tough newspaper reporter, had to preface a conclusion to his story in *Life* with this warning: "The important thing to remember about Clifford Johnson… is that he and his wife had 10 happy years together in the farm country that he loved. These were 10 years which no one ever expected would be his to live through at all." In December 1956, the now thirty-four-year-old Johnson was working as a park warden when his truck crashed into a ditch and rolled over, pinning him and spraying him with gasoline. Gas also hit the hot engine and ignited, engulfing the car. "And so Clifford Johnson died a terrible death by fire."

Martin Sheridan came to believe he was indestructible. He was hospitalized for two months, fighting off a series of life-threatening infections and complications. He received so many shots, he began to feel like a colander. Skin was shaved from his thighs to create grafts for his hands. Nurses had to spend two hours every day removing scabs from his face, neck and ear. A photograph of Sheridan's severely compromised hands was printed in the publication "Management of the Cocoanut Grove Burns at Massachusetts General Hospital"; it is painful just to look at the photo of his nearly rigid fingers. He had thirty physical therapy treatments starting in January. "On the morning of January 25, 1943—60 days, seven blood transfusions, and two skin grafts after the fire—my hands and face were nearly healed and I was ready for discharge, subject to additional skin grafting on my hands," Sheridan wrote. He was ordered to wear white gloves to keep infection from his still healing hands. He printed up cards he passed out liberally when asked about the gloves: "Not that it's any of your damn business, but my hands were burned in the Cocoanut Grove and don't ask any more questions!!" He continued to have skin grafts for months.

After a period of depression, he decided that after surviving a fire like that in the Cocoanut Grove, there was only one thing to do: go to the front and cover the war. At this point, he didn't fear death; he felt he could do anything. He got credentialed as a war correspondent and accompanied a Coast Guard cutter to Casablanca, North Africa. On a trip back home for more skin grafts, he met a young woman named Margaret Ann Cooke who was planning to volunteer for the Red Cross. Marry me instead, he said, and she did ten days later. Soon after, he took off for Greenland. But he wanted to be at the center of the action. "You hear a lot about Europe. You don't hear much about the Philippines and Japan," he told his *Boston Globe* editor. "Send me there." His editor complied.

By October 1943, he was in the Pacific theater, where he remained for the rest of the war. He spent his time dodging bullets, looking for men from New England and filing his reports under extreme deadline pressure. He would accompany the seventh wave of the 96th Division led by Douglas MacArthur on Leyte Beach. He went on a 1,500-mile bombing mission on a B-24 Liberator. He was the only correspondent to go along with a fleet of B-29s on the low-level firebombing of Tokyo and catch sight of a scene of destruction that took his breath away. Due to the distance and weight restrictions, he was told no parachutes would be on board. That was fine with Marty, who figured he would continue to outrun fate. During the raid, he drank a beer and dropped the empty Schlitz bottle into the bomb bay—it was his contribution to the war effort. He would later be the only civilian war correspondent permitted on a submarine war patrol during World War II, where he got the nickname "Scoop Sheridan." He would write a book, *Overdue and Presumed Lost* about the USS *Bullhead*, the last ship lost in World War II.

One incident stands out. Aboard the USS *Fremont* in October 1944, nine thousand miles from home, he was approached by a young sailor, who asked, "Are you Martin Sheridan?"

"Who wants to know?" Sheridan replied.

"I'm the guy who pulled you out of the Cocoanut Grove fire," said Howard Sotherden, now an electrician's mate, first class. He had been on a weekend pass from the Navy Fire Department when he joined in with the rescue work. On his final trip into the smoking club, he found a man lying face-down and moaning. When he carried him out, he heard some reporters exclaim, "Why it's Marty Sheridan." By coincidence, Sheridan had ended up on Sotherden's ship. The pair became lifelong friends.

After the war, Sheridan pursued a writing and public relations career in Chicago; he eventually retired to Connecticut. He had children, and his children had children. Every major anniversary of the fire, even sixty years later, he badgered editors about writing on the lessons of the Cocoanut Grove. He found great irony in his sudden popularity after the February 2003 Station nightclub fire in Rhode Island, when a new breed of reporters called him for comment. Until his death at age eighty-nine, Sheridan would not let a major anniversary of the fire pass without writing an article or hounding Boston media about acknowledging the Grove fire.

He never forgot, and he never wanted Boston to forget.

11

THE LEGACY OF THE COCOANUT GROVE

Among the generation that was young in 1942, it is difficult to find anyone who did not know somebody who was at the Cocoanut Grove on the night of November 28, 1948.
—*Book jacket, Paul Benzaquin,* Holocaust! The Shocking Story of the Boston Cocoanut Grove Fire, *1959*

A brass plaque, corroded by New England's hard winters, is lodged in the sidewalk along Piedmont Street in the quaint Bay Village neighborhood of Boston. Aside from this and a small historical marker on a stark blank wall nearby, the block shows no evidence of the gaiety and horror of that terrible Saturday night in November 1942.

After the club was torn down, a hotel complex was built over what was once the new lounge, and Broadway now ends at Piedmont Street. Shawmut Street Extension was built connecting Piedmont with Shawmut Street over the club footprint. For decades, an iron fence marked off a parking lot that covered the main dining room and Caricature Bar.

For the commemoration of the fiftieth anniversary of the fire, a plaque was installed at approximately the location of the revolving doors. The declaration etched into the metal is somber but concludes on an almost disconcertingly upbeat note. "Phoenix out of the Ashes," it reads, under a diagram of the doomed nightclub, dotted with little palm trees. "In memory of the more than 490 people who died as a result of the fire....As a result of this terrible tragedy major changes were made in the fire codes and improvements in the treatment of burn victims, not only in Boston

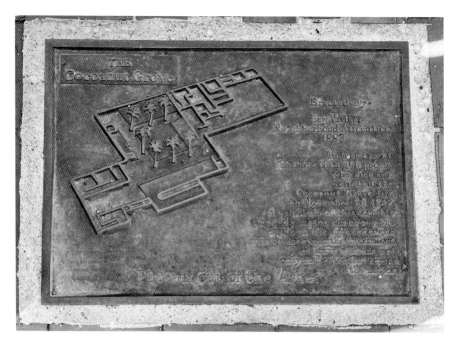

A plaque designed by Anthony "Tony" Marra, who at age fifteen was the youngest survivor of the fire, was installed in the sidewalk on Piedmont Street in 1993 for the fiftieth anniversary of the fire. The location was meant to be near the site of the revolving doors. The plaque was moved in 2016 about a block away to accommodate the building of condos on the nightclub's footprint. *Photo by author.*

but across the nation." Sometimes bouquets of flowers appear near the plaque—mute testimony of those paying tribute to the dead. Like so many aspects of this fire, even this plaque has its own contentious history. It was created by Anthony "Tony" Marra, the youngest survivor of the fire, and installed by the Bay Village Neighborhood Association. The former busboy had become a metal worker; he attended a fiftieth anniversary ceremony with other survivors, family members and city officials.

More than twenty years later, in 2013, Shawmut Street Extension was renamed Cocoanut Grove Lane through the efforts of a determined group of activists. Leading this push to honor the fire's victims was Dr. Kenneth Marshall, the son of Mary Creagh, the Boston City Hospital nurse who treated victims of the Cocoanut Grove, including Clifford Johnson. A former chief of plastic surgery at Mount Auburn Hospital in Cambridge and a clinical assistant professor of surgery at Harvard Medical School, Dr. Marshall is keenly aware of the medical breakthroughs of the fire, including burn and lung treatments, mental health, the use of penicillin

The family of Anthony P. Marra, who survived the fire and made the plaque that was installed at the site in 1992, attended the 2013 dedication of Cocoanut Grove Lane. *Photo by author.*

and the establishment of hospital blood banks. Other activists included Michael Hanlon, a lifelong civil servant in the administrations of Boston mayor Kevin White and Mayor Raymond Flynn; and Paul Miller, a resident of Bay Village who has been involved with various museums, nonprofits and charities that promote historic preservation, underserved communities and the arts. Like Martin Sheridan, they were determined that the fire not be forgotten.

The November 30, 2013 street-renaming ceremony was marked with a positive, upbeat spirit. For many, it was a cathartic event. Survivors, including Ann Clark Gallagher, Marshall Cole and John Rizzo, spoke; it was the first time Ann had returned to the site of the club. The family of Tony Marra, who had since died, were on hand. Newly elected Boston mayor Marty Walsh appeared. Cole chatted with John Rizzo and learned—after seventy years—that the man who had crashed through a window the night of the fire and jumped off the roof was a waiter who survived the fall. This waiter may have also been the man in the tuxedo that John Quinn saw running into the Melody Lounge with a fire extinguisher.

Cocoanut Grove Lane is one way to mark the fire; other legacies abound. Legislatures around the county passed fire safety code reforms in the wake of the disaster. Four days after the blaze, fire regulations were changed in St. Louis, Miami, Cleveland, Philadelphia, Detroit, Des Moines, Chicago, Kansas City, Albany, New York and Helena, Montana, according to a

Above: A radiant Ann Clark Gallagher (*center*) seated next to her sister, Carol (*right*), who lost both their parents in the fire, during the 2013 ceremony that dedicated the newly named Cocoanut Grove Lane in Boston's Bay Village neighborhood. *Photo by author.*

Right: Dr. Kenneth A. Marshall at the 2013 dedication ceremony for the naming of Cocoanut Grove Lane to honor the memory of the fire. *Photo by author.*

United Press report. Today, most states or municipalities enforce detailed egress requirements, such as requiring every revolving door be flanked by regular swing doors or have such a door nearby. Exit doors must remain unlocked from the inside and must swing in the direction of exit travel. Exits must provide a clear path to the outside. Exit signs must be clearly marked. Emergency lights must have an independent power source. No place of public assembly should be filled beyond its authorized capacity, and such places must have at least two or more exits. In addition, no combustible material should be used for decorations.

One of the lingering misconceptions about the fire is that it sparked the creation of many new fire safety codes. Rather, even prior to 1942, the National Fire Protection Association had an established recommended model egress code that covered details such as exits, crowd capacity and door type. The NFPA already considered revolving doors a "menace." According to Casey Grant, the retired executive director of the NFPA's Fire Protection Research Foundation, today's widely used "Life Safety Code" originated from the Triangle Shirtwaist Factory fire of 1911, and the Cocoanut Grove fire did not result in significant changes to the NFPA's Building Exit Code (as it was called in 1942), which already addressed the types of hazards present at the club.

What the fire did accomplish was to inspire more municipalities, Boston foremost among them, to insist on stricter application and enforcement of model codes already available. As NFPA technical secretary Robert Moulton said, Boston's building codes were, at the time of the fire, in a "chaotic condition." In 1943, Massachusetts created the Massachusetts Board of Fire Prevention Regulations, which required municipal fire officials to enforce tougher state codes. The Boston Fire Department also established a position of department chemist to evaluate draperies and decorations used in nightclubs, among other duties. Thus, the legacy of the Cocoanut Grove fire for national fire and safety codes was, in large part, centered on civic consciousness and renewed commitment to safety; the fire made lawmakers more willing to adopt national recommendations.

There was also one notable but somewhat obscure change. Prior to the fire, nightclubs were not considered places of public assembly, which are subject to more stringent codes for exits, emergency lighting, occupancy and other safety features. After the fire, nightclubs were reclassified as "places of assembly," which they obviously were. This was an unfortunate gap in regulations that had been a carryover from Prohibition, when nightclubs did not even legally exist.

It has been widely reported, even by my previous book, that the Boston Licensing Board ruled that no place of entertainment in the city could ever again use the name Cocoanut Grove. Attorney John Esposito could not find evidence that such a rule was passed, nor has Grove researcher David Blaney. Michael Hanlon, a veteran Boston civil servant, told me that this "ruling" was more of an "understanding" that was meant to prevent any party in Boston from taking advantage of the tragedy. So far, no one has tried. The Cocoanut Grove nightclub in the Ambassador Hotel in Los Angeles, California, continued to operate until it was closed in 1989 and the hotel demolished in 2006.

The medical legacy of the Cocoanut Grove has been well documented. "From the perspective of 50 years…it is apparent that the fire at the Cocoanut Grove will remain one of the most important single events in the development of burn prevention and treatment in this century," wrote Dr. Jeffrey R. Saffle in his 1993 paper on the fire published in the *American Journal of Surgery*. Boston City Hospital is now the Boston Medical Center, and the burn unit at Massachusetts General Hospital is known as the country's premier site for the treatment of burns and other fire-related injuries. Post-traumatic stress counseling is now offered to those in the military, the fire service, law enforcement and the public. It is no longer considered a sign of weakness to suffer mentally after a horrible event. We don't tell people to "just get over it" anymore.

The fire had a lasting effect on nurses who cared for its survivors. After graduating from Boston City Hospital, nurse Anne Montgomery Hargreaves enlisted in the army and was deployed with the 135th Evacuation Hospital in France and Germany, according to Barbara Poremba. She cared for young soldiers who were physically wounded by war and suffering from emotional injuries labeled "shell shock" These experiences left a profound effect on her and led her to her life's work in the field of mental health, where she pioneered the use of group dynamics. Decades later, in 1972, Hargreaves was appointed assistant deputy commissioner of Boston City Hospital and the city's Department of Health and Hospitals. The following year, when a Delta Airlines plane crashed in the fog at Boston's Logan Airport, killing all eighty-nine passengers, she called on her Grove experiences to meet the needs of grieving families, creating the basis for instituting psychiatric nurse counseling in emergency departments, according to Poremba.

The 1942 Boston College–Holy Cross game lives on in infamy—at least if you're a Boston College football fan. Kathy Dullea Hogan of Quincy found out just how much the game meant when she discovered her father's diary in a desk drawer and shared it with me. To honor her uncle who attended to victims at the fire, in 1996 she began raising money for the Reverend Maurice V. Dullea, SJ '17 Scholarship Fund. This awards a grant annually to a promising Boston College athlete from the greater Boston area.

The American rite of exorcism—the court trial—took down only one man: Barney Welansky. Even amid the calls for accountability, the public and press did not single out those "whose names you won't have to ask for how to spell." "People preferred to attack the entire administration set-up rather than certain specific individuals," wrote the authors of "The Cocoanut Grove Fire: A Study in Scapegoating" in the *Journal of Abnormal and Social Psychology* in 1943. The authors' fears that the fire would spark a wave of anti-Semitism in Boston (the Welanskys were Jewish) proved unfounded.

Yet the cynics and writers of letters to the editor were correct: those who wined and dined for free at the club were never named, much less called to account. For all his vows to "blow the lid" off the Cocoanut Grove, reporter Austen Lake uncovered little besides a sordid, colorful history described in an extravagant style. He fingered no contemporary politicians or officials; he never identified the people who made threats against him, claiming to "know who they were." As Moulton noted sarcastically in his analysis, "City officials, owners of the property, operators of the nightclub and all others who would ordinarily be held responsible have been beautifully exonerated." Welansky, languishing in jail, told a visiting Frank Shapiro, the lawyer working on compensation for survivors, "I was the victim, Frank. I took the blame for the powers and authority at the time." Author Paul Benzaquin believes Welansky was no more corrupt than any other well-connected Bostonian. "He knew the political system. He knew what he could get by on. He used the road that was there," he told me.

Five years before he died, Philip Deady, who had played a major role in investigating the fire, burned all his remaining notes on the case. His son Jack, who has also become a historian of the fire, speculates that he kept the material as "insurance" for years and wonders why his father felt the need to destroy what he had saved for so long.

In August 2004, I sat in the Boston law offices of Friedman and Atherton with ninety-five-year-old attorney Frank H. Shapiro, who was still practicing. As we talked about the fire, Shapiro would occasionally shiver, groan and put his hands over his face as tears came to his eyes. Images of pulling bodies from the fire still woke him from sleep, still haunted his dreams. "When I get up at night, I think of it. I shudder and try to brush it aside, just like you'd like to close the darkness out," he told me. Despite requests from reporters over the years, Shapiro refused to discuss all he knew about the "people behind the people behind the people involved" in the case; keeping his mouth shut, he believed, kept him alive. And now, "What good would it do?"

There has been a code of silence around the fire. Firefighter Charles Kenney, whose career was ended by the fire, never spoke much about it, not even to his son, Charles C. Kenney Jr., who was seventeen at the time and had visited his father in the hospital. Kenney Jr. would also become a firefighter, until he, like his father, suffered a career-ending injury. Late in life, Charles Kenney Jr. turned his considerable energy into researching the Cocoanut Grove fire. He began gathering material on the fire, focusing on the role of the firefighters. He collected documents, some of which he said had been discarded by the Boston Fire Department, and interviewed fellow jakes and other witnesses. He believed that the use of methyl chloride in the refrigerator unit was the accelerant that fueled the fireball that raced through the club and burned itself out. "It always bothered my father that the official cause of the fire and why it moved with such murderous speed has never been determined," wrote Charles Jr.'s son, the third to be named Charles Kenney, an author and former journalist for the *Boston Globe*, in his family memoir, *Rescue Men*. "The Cocoanut Grove fire defined our family in a way. It was as Sonny [my father] once put it, the magnetic center of our attractions to firefighting." Charles C. Kenney clung to the idea that there were additional mysteries—if not conspiracies—about Welansky's ownership and running of the club. It was almost an article of faith for him that something so terrible could only result from malfeasance in the shadows. It was, perhaps, another way to inject meaning into the pointless deaths of so many innocent people.

When I began researching the Cocoanut Grove and other fires, Charles Kenney Jr. very graciously shared his research with me. Many times I drove the traffic-choked miles from the Boston area to his home on Cape Cod to talk for hours. Charlie, drawing on his ever-present cigarette, was an engaging raconteur if sometimes frustrating source for a researcher who wanted him to get to the point. I can still sense that smoke in my nostrils as Charlie spun out stories of King Solomon, Welansky, Knocko McCormack and the myriad players in Boston's political and social scene. I think he got a huge kick out of a neophyte reporter trying to learn about firefighting while trying not to choke on his cigarette smoke. After he decided he would not write his own book, I was eager to make sure his research was preserved. With the permission of his son, I was able to get his material— which includes the club's ledger kept by Ruth Gnecco Ponzi, his interviews,

Tucked away in Boston's Bay Village is a sidewalk plaque below a street sign for Cocoanut Grove Lane, near the location of the doomed nightclub. This and a historical marker on a nearby building are the city's only public monuments to the 1942 fire. *Photo by author.*

documents and a sample of cloth that he believed was from the ceiling of the Melody Lounge—donated to the Boston Public Library, where it is available to future researchers. Kenney passed away in January 2016 at age ninety. He had served on a submarine in the Pacific in World War II, and his ashes were scattered in the waters near Pearl Harbor.

Charlie would have been angry, but not surprised, when the small parking lot on the footprint of the club was sold for the development of luxury condominiums. The developers asked that Marra's plaque, which was in the sidewalk near the property, be removed temporarily; then they requested it be permanently moved. Reaction was swift and furious; the developers were accused of being insensitive to a tragic event in Boston history. Eventually, the plaque was moved about a block away and now is located under the sign for Cocoanut Grove Lane. This incident further galvanized a group of people, including Dr. Marshall, Hanlon, Miller, David Blaney, Barbara Poremba, former Boston Fire Department commissioner Paul Christian and others, to push for building a larger, appropriate memorial for the fire, one that would honor the dead and stand as a teaching reference for a new generation. The Cocoanut Grove Memorial Committee, a registered 501(c) (3) not-for-profit organization, was established in 2015. "Our objective is to create a memorial that preserves and honors the memory of the victims, survivors, first responders and medical professionals," according to the organization's website, www.cocoanutgrove.org.

As of this writing, Boston has granted approval for a memorial in Statler Park, a small green space that is just a few blocks from where the club stood. Funds have been raised, and fundraising is ongoing. A design based on the multiple archway entrance of the nightclub is in the works.

In April 2022, I met with Michael Hanlon at a restaurant in the Charlestown neighborhood of Boston to ask him, bluntly, why does Boston need a memorial to this event? Shouldn't we just put this horror behind us? "Boston is a city of history and also a city of innovations, a leader in education, a leader in law, a leader in medical practice. All those things are intertwined with the Cocoanut Grove fire," he told me. "What we're trying to do is really preserve this chapter in Boston's history."

Hanlon shifted in the booth to look around the restaurant. "For instance, we're in a restaurant right now. You can see the exit sign there. And it's on its own power. And that's a direct result of the Cocoanut Grove fire.

"People may not think about this anymore. They might walk by and see the street sign saying Cocoanut Grove Lane. That may not mean anything to them. If their eyes go to the base of that street sign and they see the

This is an artist rendering of a proposed memorial for the Cocoanut Grove fire that is to be installed in Statler Park on Stuart Street in Boston, a few blocks from the site of the original club. The design mimics the archway of the entrance to the doomed club and is intended to be inscribed with the names of the victims of the fire. *Courtesy of Michael Hanlon.*

plaque, then maybe they might understand that something tragic did happen there."

Adding poignancy to the push to create a physical memorial is the sad reality that living memories of the fire are disappearing. The Cocoanut Grove Memorial Committee believes there are only two known survivors of the fire still alive as of May 2022. I had a chance to meet one of them, ninety-eight-year-old Robert L. Shumway of Naples, Florida, via Zoom during Memorial Day weekend in 2022. His son and daughter also participated in the call. (The other survivor is ninety-eight-year-old Joyce Spector Mekelburg.) Bob Shumway was a seventeen-year-old Williston Academy student in Amherst, Massachusetts, when he went with his best buddy Dick Moulton to Boston on November 28, 1942, to see the football game at Fenway Park. After the game, the pair decided to go to the Cocoanut Grove, which they had heard about. Shumway had never been in a nightclub before. But "we were young and full of it," Shumway said. "We were Williston Prep hot potatoes."

Shumway still lives on his own with twenty-four-hour care and plays gin with buddies, but the memories of what happened in the club have almost disappeared. He had previously told his family that he and Dick were in the club for about a half hour hanging out at the Caricature Bar when they saw what looked like an explosion roar through the club. The young men managed to get out through the club's revolving doors without injury, and they stayed for an hour trying to help other people escape. He now doesn't recall how he got out, but he does clearly remember how dangerous revolving doors can be. "You have got to learn to push the right side of it. Push both sides of it and nobody gets anywhere," he said. "Ever since then, when I go to a place and it gets [crowded] with a lot of people, I always look for an exit and see where they are before anything happens."

He said he still wants to be "one of the first out." That saved his life nearly eighty years ago. He still remembers that.

EPILOGUE

And some things that should not have been forgotten were lost.
History became legend. Legend became myth.
—Prologue from Peter Jackson's film The Lord of the Rings,
based on the trilogy by J.R.R. Tolkien

In the weeks before I finished this book, a radio story on the local NPR station caught my ear. A reporter was talking about covering the 2017 truck bombing in Mogadishu, Somalia, that took more than five hundred lives. Five hundred lives. That number again. The NPR reporter went on in measured tones about how she wished the bombing could be seen as a tragedy of unique individuals, each person with their own life story cut short, not just as a mass casualty in a foreign country.

In the 1940s, against the backdrop of a world war with slaughter and genocide that would tax our comprehension of human cruelty, the country viewed the Cocoanut Grove fire as a mass casualty just affecting the Boston area. Many of those who survived the fire—John Quinn, Marshall Cole, Martin Sheridan and Bob Shumway, for example—would be witnesses to mass destruction on an even greater scale when they joined or accompanied the U.S. military.

Private First Class Charles J. "Buddy" McNeill of Cambridge saw the ghastliness of the Cocoanut Grove up close when he was a driver for the Technology Ambulance Services of Cambridge. He was among those assigned to remove mutilated bodies from the club. "I thought I'd see the

The front entrance of the Cocoanut Grove on Piedmont Street showing the archway that led to the revolving doors. *Army Signal Corps/Courtesy of Boston Public Library.*

worst sight of my life that Sunday morning when we started to remove bodies of fire victims," McNeill told a reporter for a Cambridge newspaper. That was before he enlisted in the army on April 3, 1942, and became a member of the 116th Evacuation Hospital, which took medical assistance to Dachau when that Nazi death camp was liberated by American forces. At the camp, he had to deal with hundreds of bodies on the ground that began to rot and people who were just barely alive. The Cocoanut Grove paled in comparison.

I know of McNeill's story because his grandson Kevin Richards of Londonderry, New Hampshire, reached out to me about his grandfather and sent an undated clipping about him. He tells me his grandfather died on March 31, 1952, from acute toxic alcoholism. He could not get over the horrors he witnessed, Richard believes. He was anxious for information on the Cocoanut Grove for his eighty-five-year-old mother, who adored her father.

Eighty years after this fire, we still see its ripple effect over generations. While the fire's impact does not begin to compare to World War II or even the September 11, 2001 terrorism attacks in New York City and Washington, D.C., the memory of this tragedy should not be allowed to fade. We should try not to let verified information be supplanted with often-told tales that may or may not be true. To paraphrase from the epigraph: in the Cocoanut Grove, facts became legends. Legends became myths. And stories that should not have been forgotten have been nearly lost. But even as the last living memories of the Cocoanut Grove disappear, the appetite for knowledge and the hunger for meaning continue.

I often end my public talks on the history of the nightclub fire with the call for support of life safety codes and regulations that—however onerous they may appear—are designed to save lives when something goes wrong. Lessons need to be repeated. Consider the 2003 Station Nightclub fire in West Warwick, Rhode Island; the 2016 Ghost Ship fire in Oakland, California; and the 2017 Grenfell Tower fire in London. I have an additional message here. It may be difficult, but can we see future disasters not in terms of death tolls or statistics but as individual stories of unique humans? Can we extend that perception to other events around the country and around the world? If so, then perhaps we can generate the compassion and determination to make our world safer.

NOTES ON SOURCES

1. Boston's Number One Glitter Spot

Background on the Cocoanut Grove from Paul Benzaquin, *Holocaust! Fire in Boston's Cocoanut Grove* (Boston: Branden Press, 1967), Edward Keyes, *Cocoanut Grove* (New York: Atheneum, 1984), Austen Lake, *Galley Slave* (Boston: Burdette and Company, 1965) and articles by Lake in the *Boston Record American*, December 1942. Edith Nussinow material from interview, January 14, 2011. Other sources are newspaper articles in the *Boston Daily Globe*, *Boston Herald*, *Boston Post*, *Boston Daily Record*, *Boston Evening American* and *Boston Traveler*, from November 1942 through January 1943. Angelo Lippi's tales are from Anthony La Camera and George Holland, "Celebrities Made Cocoanut Grove Famous and Colorful," printed in a special section of the *Boston Sunday Advertiser*, December 6, 1942. Linney's inspection report was included in John Vahey's analysis of the Cocoanut Grove fire, "Design for Disaster," published in 1982 by the Boston Sparks Association. Other details on the club from John Esposito, *Fire in the Grove: The Cocoanut Grove Tragedy and Its Aftermath* (Boston: Da Capo Press, 2006)

2. The Cowboy and the Scribe

Much of the background on Buck Jones from Joseph G. Rosa, "Buck Jones Bona Fide Hero," *True West*, August 1966, also Donald Liebeson, "Nostalgia

Packed, Universal Dusts off Three Westerns of the Cowboy Hero Buck Jones," *Chicago Tribune*, January 1, 1998, and Doug Nye, "A Cloud of Dust… Cowboys of Our Youth Fast Heading for the Last Roundup," *Chicago Tribune*, January 21, 2000. Other sources: Dorothy Wayman, "Buck Jones Hospital Tour Helped Little Boy to Health," *Boston Globe*, December 1, 1942; Paul Wait, Commander in Chief, "Solemn Services for Buk Jones," *Boston Traveler*, December 4, 1942; "Buck Jones Is Dead of Injuries in Fire," *New York Times*, November 30, 1942; "Buck Jones Fan Club Seeks to Lasso Stamp for Late Cowboy Star," *San Diego Union-Tribune*, June 1, 1989; "Buck Jones to Play Villain Roles in Film," UPI, April 23, 1940; and Elliot Norton, "Cowboy Star Dies of Burns," *Boston Post*, December 1, 1942. Details on Martin Sheridan from November 14, 2002, interview at his home in Connecticut; interview with his daughter, Meg Schmidt, by Zoom, April 15, 2022, and essays written by Sheridan, including, "I Survived the Cocoanut Grove Disaster," dated July 27, 1943, and the unpublished essay "The Extraordinary Life of Martin Sheridan," by Meg Schmidt.

3. The Debacle at Fenway Park

Ned Dullea's diary courtesy of his daughter, Kathy Dullea Hogan, who provided other materials. Other details are based on interviews with Martin Sheridan and John Quinn (November 11, 2010), Frank Shapiro (September 3, 2004) and Ann Clark Gallagher (August 24, 2014). Goody Goodelle from her own account posted at https://contrafactual.com/2013/12/02/goody-goodelle/ and interview with daughter Nora Bergman, April 15, 2022. Dorothy Myles from "I Almost Burned to Death," *True Experiences*, October 1948. Jack Lesberg from Phillip Atteberry, "Jack Lesberg: Bassist Extraordinaire: Jazz and the Classics Do Mix," brochure, "The March of Jazz" 2003. Also "Inferno at the Cocoanut Grove," *Yankee*, November 1998; Judy Bass, "No Way Out," *Boston Magazine*, October 1992.

4. Into the Inferno

Sheridan from November 14, 2002 interview. Details of Stanley Tomaszewski and Daniel Weiss from Charles C. Kenney papers. Vera Daniels from letter in Kenney papers and "Inferno at the Cocoanut Grove," *Yankee*, November 1998. Ann Clark from interview, August 24, 2014. Mickey Alpert, Billy Payne from Benzaquin, *Holocaust!*, Jack Lesberg from Phillip D. Atteberry. Dotty Myles from "I Almost Burned to Death," *True Experiences*, October 1948. John Quin, *Yankee*, November 1998, and interview 2003 and video interview November 11, 2010. Marshall Cole, interview, November 30, 2013, and www.cocoanutgrove.org. John Rizzo, from documentary *Six Locked Doors*, written and produced by Zachary Graves-Miller. Goody Goodelle, from her own account posted at https://contrafactual.com/2013/12/02/goody-goodelle/ and interview with daughter Nora Bergman, April 15, 2022. John H. Senft's account from his statement to police, November 30, 1942; see https://archive.org/search.php?query=cocoanut%20grove%20fire%20 AND%20collection%3Aamericana. Other details from John Vahey's analysis of the Cocoanut Grove fire, "Design for Disaster," published in 1982 by the Boston Sparks Association; Robert Moulton's 1943 NFPA report; "Looking Back at the Cocoanut Grove," *Fire Journal*, November 1982; William Arthur Reilly, fire commissioner, city of Boston, "Report Concerning the Cocoanut Grove Fire," November 19, 1943, https://archive.org/details/reportconcerning00bost/page/n11/mode/2up. Also witness statements from the Boston Police Department archive and Boston newspaper accounts from November 29 to December 11, 1942; "'Bubbles' Shea, Giant Grove Bartender Dies," *Boston Globe*, February 18, 1943.

5. Fighting the Fire

Information on the Luongo Fire in East Boston from the Boston Fire Historical Society website, www.bostonfirehistory.org. Details on how the Cocoanut Grove fire was fought is based on interviews with Charles C. Kenney and Jack Deady in 2003; John Vahey's analysis of the Cocoanut Grove fire, "Design for Disaster"; Casey Cavanaugh Grant, "Last Dance at the Cocoanut Grove," *NFPA Journal*, May/June 1991. Graney account is based on his unpublished interview with Charles C. Kenney and Grant, "Last Dance at the Cocoanut Grove." Accounts of Patrick "Joe" Connolly and Johnny Rose based on unpublished interviews by Charles C. Kenney. John Collins's account is from Grant, "Last Dance." Dotty Myles's account from "After 18 Years, Singer Recalls Cry of, 'Fire,' at Cocoanut Grove," *New York World Telegram and Sun*, December 27, 1960. Details on the career of Charles Kenney Sr. from *Rescue Men* (New York: Public Affairs, 2007), a family memoir by Charles Kenney (the third). Other details on companies and alarms from www.bostonfirehistory.org.

6. Treating the Victims

Sources for this chapter: Barbara Ravage, *Burn Unit: Saving Lives after the Flames* (Boston: Da Capo Press, 2004); Symposium on the Management of the Cocoanut Grove Burns at the Massachusetts General Hospital, 1943, edited by Dr. Oliver Cope and containing fifteen articles from different disciplines on all aspects of the fire, originally published in *Annals of Surgery* 117 (1943); Maxwell Finland, Charles S. Davidson and Stanley M. Levenson, "Clinical and Therapeutic Aspects of the Conflagration Injuries to the Respiratory Tract Sustained by Victims of the Cocoanut Grove Disaster," *Medicine* 25 (1946): 215–83; Finland, Davidson and Levenson, "Effects of Plasma and Fluid on Pulmonary Complications in Burned Patients: Studies of the Effects in Victims of the Cocoanut Grove," *Archives of Internal Medicine* 77, no. 5 (May 1946); Francis Moore, *A Miracle and a Privilege* (Washington, D.C.: National Academy Press, 1995); Atul Gawande, "Desperate Measures," *New Yorker*, May 5, 2003; Oliver Cope, "The End of the Tannic Acid Era," and Thomas H. Coleman, "A Hush on the Brick Corridor," both in the *Harvard Medical Alumni Bulletin*, Winter 1991/1992; "Inferno at the Cocoanut Grove," *Yankee*, November 1998; John C. Sheehan and Robert N. Ross, "The Fire that Made Penicillin Famous," *Yankee*, November 1982; Gloria Negri, "A Wing and a Prayer Reunion," *Boston Globe*, November 14, 1994; S.B. Levy, "From Tragedy the Antibiotic Age Is Born," in *The Antibiotic Paradox* (Boston: Springer, 1992); Jeffry R. Saffle, MD, FAC, "The 1942 Fire at Boston's Cocoanut Grove Nightclub," *American Journal of Surgery* 166 (December 1993). Also, letter from John H.T. McPherson Jr. to friends and family describing his experience treating victims of the Cocoanut Grove nightclub fire, see https://www.digitalcommonwealth.org/search/commonwealth-oai:fq979h63. Information on nurses at the Cocoanut Grove is largely based on a May 6, 2022 interview and subsequent correspondence with Barbara Poremba, who shared her research. Mental health innovations from Erich Lindemann, "Symptomatology and Management of Acute Grief," *American Journal of Psychiatry* 101 (1944).

7. As the Ashes Cooled

Details on funerals from http://genealogytrails.com/mass/suffolk/news_cocoanutgrove_obits.html and issues of the *Boston Globe* November to December 1942. Buck Jones from Rosa, "Buck Jones Bona Fide Hero"; Trem Carr's hyped tribute to Jones in "Final Honors to Buck Jones," AP December 8, 1942; "Buck Jones Bond Drive Inaugurated," *Richmond Times-Dispatch*, February 15, 1943. Knocko McCormack story from Garrison Nelson, *John William McCormack: A Political Biography* (New York: Bloomsbury, 2017), and WBUR interview with Nelson at https://www.wbur.org/radioboston/2017/06/27/john-mccormack-bio. Material on African Americans in the fire from Jim Hewlett, "Color Bar Saves Lives of Negroes in Boston's Tragic Cocoanut Grove Fire," *Detroit Tribune*, December 12, 1942, and "Mr. Plenty Dies in Grove Fire: Mrs. Daniels is Injured Seriously," *Boston Chronicle*, December 5, 1942, provided by David Blaney. Information on death toll from interviews and correspondence with David Blaney, April to May 2022. Other details on deaths and injuries from the "Facts about the Cocoanut Grove Nightclub," by David Blaney, posted on the website of the Cocoanut Grove Memorial committee, www.cocoanutgrove.org

8. The Investigation and Trial

Details on the investigation from transcripts of the Reilly hearings, provided by Charles C. Kenney and reported by the press. Boston Police interviews at https://archive.org/search.php?query=cocoanut%20grove%20fire%20AND%20collection%3Aamericana. Details on the trial from stories in the *Boston Herald, Globe, Post, Traveler, Record American, Advertiser* and the *Christian Science Monitor*. Also "Venerable Lawyer Still Holds Secret to Famed '42 Fire," *Massachusetts Lawyers Weekly*, June 2, 1997. Analysis from John Esposito, *Fire in the Grove: The Cocoanut Grove Tragedy and Its Aftermath* (Boston: Da Capo Press, 2005). "Rudnick Paroled from State Prison," *Boston Globe*, October 8, 1945.

9. What Caused the Fire?

Details on the timing of the fire, its speed and other facts from interview on April 22, 2022, and subsequent correspondence with Casey Grant, based on a presentation on October 18, 2021, in Baltimore, Maryland, at the 2021 SFPE Annual Meeting. Also, numerous interviews with Charles C. Kenney and Jack Deady in 2003–4; research notes from Jack Deady, "Did a Mystery Gas Fuel the Cocoanut Grove Fire"; and Kenney's unpublished monograph

"The Initial Accelerant"; Charles Kenney, *Firehouse*, May 1999; Doug Beller and Jennifer Sapochetti, "Searching for Answer to the Cocoanut Grove Fire of 1942," *NFPA Journal*, May/June 2000.

10. The Struggle to Recover

Interviews with Martin Sheridan; Meg Schmidt, Nora Berman and Jane Alpert Bouvier. Details of Clifford Johnson from Paul Benzaquin, "Youth's Fearful Ordeal by Fire," *Life*, August 31, 1959; Benzaquin, *Holocaust!*, and interview with Paul Benzaquin, August 15, 2004. I am indebted to David Blaney for his research on the alleged Boston College victory party at the Cocoanut Grove. Weiss details from Charles C. Kenney material and Dunlap from Paul Benzaquin, *Holocaust!*

11. The Legacy of the Cocoanut Grove

Sources include interviews with Michael Hanlon (April 2, 2022), Ken Marshall (May 11, 2022), Frank Shapiro (August 24, 2004), Paul Benzaquin (August 15, 2004) and Casey Grant (April 23, 2022). Bob Shumway information from interview on May 28, 2022, and "Survivor Story: Bob Shumway," at www.cocoanutgrove.org. Joyce Spector details from https://www.cocoanutgrove.org/lastsurvivors. Background on the fiftieth anniversary from "Tragedy Is Commemorated: Ceremony at Cocoanut Grove Site Sees Bittersweet Reunion," *Boston Globe*, November 29, 1992; "Cocoanut Grove 50-Year Ceremony Set," *Boston Herald*, November 27, 1992.

Epilogue

"Cambridge Soldier Compares Dachau Horrors to Cocoanut Grove Fire Mutilations," undated clipping from a Cambridge newspaper.

RESOURCES

The Internet is filled with information on the Cocoanut Grove fire—some good, some dubious. For those seeking more information, I recommend these sites.

The Cocoanut Grove Memorial Committee, www.cocoanutgrove.org.
This includes research by David Blaney, who has put together a huge database of material on the fire victims.

Boston Fire Historical Society, www.bostonfirehistory.org
In particular, see the special Cocoanut Grove sections:
   https://bostonfirehistory.org/the-story-of-the-cocoanut-grove-fire/
   https://bostonfirehistory.org/archives-artifacts/archives/cocoanut-
      grove-fire-special-section/
This site contains scans of material gathered by Charles C. Kenney.

The National Fire Protection Association and collaborators,
   https://sites.google.com/view/cocoanutgrove-fire./
This site features original and secondary sources.

The website for *Six Locked Doors: Legacy of Cocoanut Grove*,
   www.sixlockeddoors.com.
This has links and information about the making of this documentary.

INDEX

ABOUT THE AUTHOR

S tephanie Schorow is a journalist, writing instructor and the author or coauthor of eight books on Boston history: *The Great Boston Fire: The Inferno that Nearly Incinerated the City*; *Inside the Combat Zone: The Stripped Down Story of Boston's Most Notorious Neighborhood*; *Drinking Boston: A History of the City and Its Spirits*; *Boston on Fire: A History of Fires and Firefighting in Boston*; *East of Boston: Notes from the Harbor Island*; *The Crime of the Century: How the Brink's Robbers Stole Millions and the Hearts of Boston*; and, with Beverly Ford, *The Boston Mob Guide: Hitmen, Hoodlum and Hideouts*. She has worked as an editor and reporter for the *Boston Herald*, the Associated Press and newspapers in Connecticut, Idaho and Utah.